D1409596

Believe in the
possibilities!

Smiles....

"When I was about to hurtle down Calgary's Olympic bobsleigh track in 2013 in a contraption that looked no stronger than a soft-drink can, Heather put her hand on my shoulder and said, 'This will be fun and you can do it.' That gold-medal–winning touch (and the fact she sat right behind me in the bobsled) gave me confidence—just like this book will do for you. It's smart, inspiring, and incredibly thoughtful, with a lesson about your potential and how to reach it on every page."

PETER MANSBRIDGE

"Heather's connection to a rich life is laced with winning and risk and love. I admire her as much for conversations over a beer in Summerside, P.E.I., as I do for the post–Olympic-gold-medal interview in Sochi, Russia. There are so many people steering our lives, but only one applying the brakes. In her book, Heather shows you how to release those brakes, stop at nothing, and go all the way."

RON MACLEAN, host of *Hockey Night in Canada* and *Rogers Hometown Hockey*

"*Redefining 'Realistic'* is a personal invitation from Heather Moyse to you to realize your potential and to nurture the potential in others. She is a contemporary authority on mind over matter and a relevant voice in the wilderness as she sets out to help you redefine realistic and seize your potential. A must-read for parents, teachers, and leaders."

SUZANNE BALCOM, life coach and professional speaker

"At some point in our lives, we are all healing from something or other. Heather Moyse's *Redefining 'Realistic'* is a must-read for anyone rehabilitating from a physical or psychological injury or facing a challenge or seemingly insurmountable obstacle. This is a wonderfully readable book filled with wisdom that only someone who has challenged adversity could garner. Heather brings us back to basics when it comes to charting the course of our lives. An inspiring manual for owning your story."

LCOL MARKUS BESEMANN, CD, BSC, MD, FRCP(C), DIP SPORT MED, Chief of Rehabilitation Medicine for the Canadian Forces Health Services and team physician for the True Patriot Love expeditions in 2012 (Nepal), 2014 (North Pole), and 2016 (Antarctica)

"Heather Moyse is an inspirational thought leader who, through her storytelling, shares stories from her life as a guide to help the reader unlock their greatest potential. In her book, *Redefining 'Realistic'*, you will find the courage to follow your own path and discover your *root why* to keep you grounded in your purpose. Heather is a true role model!"

LEANNE NICOLLE, President and CEO of Big Brothers Big Sisters, Executive in Residence at Ted Rogers School of Management, Ryerson University, and former president of the Canadian Olympic Foundation

"A shift in behaviour starts with a shift in thinking. Follow Heather's hard-earned wisdom outlined in *Redefining 'Realistic'* and discover how you can achieve the life of success you truly deserve."

BRIAN TRACY, CPAE, Chairman and CEO of Brian Tracy International, speaker, author, and trainer

"Heather Moyse is living proof that anything is possible. As an athlete, I watched her demonstrate in the most powerful way that you create your own reality. In *Redefining 'Realistic'*, Heather shows that there are no limits when you truly believe and move forward with curiosity to see what is possible. We can all learn from her phenomenal experiences, achievements, and perspective to move forward with an openness that will allow us to reach our own goals and dreams."

CLARA HUGHES, OC (Order of Canada), OM (Order of Manitoba), and six-time Olympic medallist, cycling and speed skating

"Heather is one of the most engaging and motivating people one could ever encounter. Her infectious, relentlessly upbeat mindset and perspective helped all of us as we struggled to climb the highest summit in Antarctica by focusing beyond the adversity to the possible and creating self-belief. It wasn't her gold medals that dazzled but her attitude and approach. Read this book and you will come to understand where it came from and what it can mean for you. In short, you will see what I saw and be inspired as I was."

ANDY CHISHOLM, investor, philanthropist, and former Goldman Sachs partner

"It is one thing to write about a topic, quite another to actually live it every day—Heather Moyse does both. Do not delay—read this book and discover how you can achieve the life of success you truly deserve."

JOSEPH SHERREN, bestselling author, Canadian Hall of Fame Speaker, and professor at York University Business School

"Heather Moyse is a true-to-herself athlete. In *Redefining 'Realistic'*, Heather has put into words just what I needed to hear. This book will encourage young and old alike to look differently at the possibilities in their lives and to overcome the obstacles that may be standing in their way. I now see more possibilities for myself even after twenty years on the LPGA tour. Thanks, Heather! You really do inspire greatness! A gold-medal read!"

LORIE KANE, CM (Order of Canada), Canadian Golf Hall-of-Famer, and member of the Ladies Professional Golf Association (LPGA)

REDEFINING
'REALISTIC'

HEATHER MOYSE

REDEFINING

'REALISTIC'

Shift Your Perspective,
Seize Your Potential,
Own Your Story.

RR RED ROOTS PUBLISHING

Copyright © 2017 by Heather Moyse

All rights reserved. No part of this book may be reproduced,
stored in a retrieval system or transmitted, in any form or by
any means, except in the case of reviews, without the prior written
consent of the publisher or a licence from The Canadian Copyright
Licensing Agency (Access Copyright). For a copyright licence, visit
www.access-copyright.ca or call toll free to 1-800-893-5777.

Red Roots Publishing
Toronto ON
bookqueries@heathermoyse.com
www.heathermoyse.com

Cataloguing data available from Library and Archives Canada
ISBN 978-1-7750972-2-8 (hardcover)
ISBN 978-1-7750972-0-4 (paperback)
ISBN 978-1-7750972-1-1 (ebook)
ISBN 978-1-7750972-3-5 (audiobook)

Produced by Page Two
www.pagetwostrategies.com
Design by Peter Cocking
Printed and bound in Canada by Friesens

17 18 19 20 21   5 4 3 2 1

I dedicate this book to those who've been told they can't;

To those who have a goal that is beyond the
limited vision of others;

To those who are striving to reach their potential,
and to those who have already achieved success and
use it to empower others; and, finally...

To Mom and Dad—for instilling in me a sense
of perspective and a belief in the possibilities
that have been essential to my own achievements,
and now enable me to help others achieve
their goals. Without you, this book would not
have been possible.

"To laugh often and much; to win the respect of intelligent people and the affection of children; to earn the appreciation of honest critics and endure the betrayal of false friends; to appreciate the beauty, to find the best in others; to leave the world a bit better, whether by a healthy child, a garden patch or a redeemed social condition; to know even one life has breathed easier because you have lived. This is to have succeeded."

A POPULAR ADAPTATION OF THE POEM "SUCCESS" BY BESSIE ANDERSON STANLEY

CONTENTS

FOREWORD

by John C. Maxwell

I HAD THE PLEASURE of meeting Heather Moyse in 2014 when I spoke to three completely different audiences at an event in Eastern Canada. Heather presented the opening keynote for each audience: six thousand high school students in a coliseum, a few dozen VIPs during a small private luncheon, and a few hundred local business and community leaders.

Rarely do I hear a speaker who connects as well to an audience as Heather does. Since our first encounter, I've had the privilege of mentoring her in her speaking career. Most excitingly, I've seen her flourish in the world of speaking and help tens of thousands of people see their potential by sharing her unique perspectives.

I am delighted that she's chosen to write this book, as it will allow her powerful messaging—of *shifting your perspective, seizing your potential*, and *owning your story*—to reach people beyond her speaking engagements and provide further insight for those who are keen for more. Heather truly wants people to reach their goals and, ultimately, fulfill their potential.

Her unique experiences—entering the world of elite sports at an older age—give her a rare perspective that she shares in these pages. Heather not only provides readers with the insight into where that perspective comes from but also helps them shift their own perspective to see and seize their potential.

She has deftly woven her personal experiences into the messaging, sharing both the exciting stories of reaching the top of the Olympic podium and the teaching moments that developed the philosophies and beliefs that helped her get there. Although she is a three-sport national athlete and two-time Olympic gold medallist, she is as relatable and as personable in this book as she is in person and on the stage.

I admire the energy that Heather brings to any room she enters, and am touched by her compassionate spirit. I have so much respect for how she's turned a successful athletic career into a vehicle for empowering others.

She is a true leader in the way she lives her life, and I feel blessed to be able to call her a friend.

A NOTE FROM
THE AUTHOR

N THE PROCESS of writing this book, I discovered both an American and British style of punctuation. Because the British style makes the most logical sense to me (and that's what my parents taught me), I have *chosen* to go against the grain of conventional publishing and use a hybrid of British and American punctuation. After all, this *is* a book about making the choices that are right for you, and not just going with the flow. ☺

Also, because I want this book to reflect the casual tone I would use if I were speaking with you in a café (or from the stage, for that matter), I am *intentionally* breaking some grammar rules. I hope that the grammar police (and my mother) will forgive me.

INTRODUCTION

WE ARE ALL CAPABLE OF *WAY MORE*

IMAGINE IF THERE was a No Parking sign on the road to your best possible self—to the fulfillment of your potential. Imagine if there weren't any Exit signs. Imagine if you weren't allowed to pull over on the side of that road. Now imagine if you were in a vehicle equipped to deal with the potholes and bumps, the washed-out bridges, the other terrible drivers, the confusing road signs and detours, and the worst weather Mother Nature could throw at you. Imagine if you *knew* you were unstoppable. Unconquerable.

Where would you end up? What would you set your sights on, what destination would you program your GPS to if you knew you had what it took to get there—the right armour, the right tires, the right amount of the right kind of fuel, the right directions, the right companions? Now, what goals would you pursue if you knew you had what it took to get *there*—the right mindset, the right skills, the right resources, the right energy, the right inner circle of support?

It's time to redefine 'realistic'!

It's not about
the guarantees.
It's about the
possibilities!

The Power of Gold

The first time I stood on top of an Olympic podium, hearing "O Canada" playing, it was hard to believe I was actually there. *Surreal* is the word I frequently use to describe that moment. As a child, I had never dreamed of being an Olympic athlete, and I didn't even consider pursuing that unlikely goal until I was persuaded by someone to try out when I was—twenty-seven years old! Since then, I trained and competed on the national team for many years, and the experience taught me a lot about myself and what I was truly capable of.

In fact, I have won Olympic gold twice; represented my country in three different sports—bobsleigh (2006, 2010, and 2014 Winter Olympics), rugby (2006 and 2010 Rugby World Cup and the 2013 Rugby World Cup Sevens), and cycling (2012 Pan American Track Cycling Championships—and in 2016 was the second Canadian ever to be inducted into the World Rugby Hall of Fame. How, you ask, could I have accomplished all that if it wasn't a lifelong dream, a burning ambition? Because I became open to the possibilities of my own potential. Because I looked at my life from a different perspective and chose to go for it.

Now I am a motivational speaker, on a mission to help other people see their own potential and live up to it—to be *way more* than they think they can be. I am constantly amazed at how viscerally my audiences respond to my two Olympic gold medals, and how inspired they are by them. Sure, they're cool—one of the ultimate and most recognizable rewards for human achievement in this world—which is why I pass them around as much as possible. I stick around after my speaking engagements for as long as I can so people can hold them and try them on. I *want* people to have their own moment with those medals (and take their selfies).

And I don't mind if I am in the photos or not. Yes, those medals are mine, but those moments aren't about *me*. Those medals are a tangible representation of each person's dreams and goals, and I want *others* to feel empowered: for one shining golden moment, to get out of their heads and back to believing in the possibilities of what *they* are truly capable of. Something powerful happens when people hold those medals: a shift in their energy, a shift in their perspective, a glimpse of what *they* might be able to achieve, a flicker of the possibilities that truly exist. Who am I to keep that from people? If I were to lock my medals in a safety deposit box and only take them out ten years from now to see them in perfect condition—untouched—I would feel ashamed of myself. If it means the gold gets a bit worn by passing them around, if the ribbons get a bit frayed, it's worth it. That kind of inspiration is worth its weight—'in gold'!

AS A SPEAKER, I have been blessed with opportunities to talk to people of all ages and interests. I have spoken to organizations around the world—from government departments to financial institutions to software and engineering companies to agricultural associations to universities and education groups to not-for-profits to major leadership conferences—and I've come to realize that the qualities it takes to be successful as an athlete are the same qualities it takes to be successful in any industry. Not only are those qualities—those traits and characteristics—the same, but so is the fact that *every* single person, job, and industry has its own unique challenges.

The best thing, in my opinion, about having won two Olympic gold medals is that it has afforded me a platform from which I can inspire and empower rooms full of people to look beyond those unique challenges and see the potential that exists within themselves and their circumstances.

The first time I was told that my message changed someone's life—that it came at just the right time, that they had *needed* to hear it—it changed *mine*. And every time I receive similar comments after a speaking engagement or from someone who has simply followed my career, it reinforces my compulsion to continue along the path of inspiring and empowering other people—as many as I possibly can.

Now, empowering others is not only a passion but also a calling for me. And I am addicted to the feeling of empowerment *I* get when I discover I've empowered someone else—that I've helped them question their assumptions, shift their perspective to see and believe in the possibilities of what they are capable of, or have ignited a passion inside of *them* to embrace challenges and discover how far *they* can go on the path to their best self.

AFTER LISTENING TO some of my personal stories of challenges, perspective, and achievement, people often ask me what my *next* goals are. I then hear words like *lofty* and *ambitious* floating around in response to what I tell them, followed by the questions "Do you really think that will happen? Do you think that's *realistic*? Do you *really* think you can accomplish that?"

Well, my answer is simple: "I have no idea. But I sure as *hell* am going to see how close I can get!"

You see, when pursuing *any* dream or goal, it's not about the guarantees. It's about the possibilities! Because there *are* no guarantees—not in sports, not in business, and not in life. There are too many things beyond our control. But believing in the possibilities allows us to focus on finding solutions; to challenge not only society's boundaries but especially our own self-limiting beliefs and behaviours that hold us back from being our best; to test the threshold of our potential and the threshold of what is possible. Going for your personal gold—pursuing your own dreams—is about embracing the challenge of seeing how *good* you can become—how *close* you can get—and discovering for yourself what is 'realistic'. I mean, nobody thought it was possible to run the four-minute mile until Roger Bannister did it in 1954, which shifted people's perspective as to the possibilities... and now people do it all the time.

One of my personal philosophies is that we are all capable of way more than we give ourselves credit for, in sports, in business, in relationships, and in life. It is my goal not only to help people realize how true that statement is but also to make them see the possibilities of what they are able to achieve in their own lives—not just in terms of performance but also fulfillment.

Redefining 'Realistic' is about human potential. More importantly, it is about *your* potential. It is about not selling yourself short, and fulfilling the possibilities that lie deep inside you—even if you can't see them yet. It addresses the obstacles to achieving your goals—both the tangible ones you can see *and* the ones you create for yourself in your own mind—the things that prevent you from moving forward and turning your dreams into realities. Basically, this book is about helping you realize that *you* are capable of *way more* than you give yourself credit for; it's about becoming the best version of yourself and living a life of personal excellence—the ultimate definition of success, as defined by you. And, yes, that means *you! You* are in the driver's seat. Shift your perspective, seize your potential—and own your story.

For additional information and resources to help get you where you want to be—to figure out what you are truly capable of—please visit me at **www.heathermoyse.com**.

PART

1

SHIFT

YOUR

PERSPECTIVE

RETURN TO OPTIMISM

REMEMBER WHEN YOU were a kid and you believed—
really believed—that you could be anything you
dreamed of becoming? A pilot, an astronaut, a
superhero, an Olympic gold medallist? Remember when you
believed you could really *do* anything you wanted? Climbing
a mountain, travelling the globe, starting your own business,
having a positive impact on the world? What allowed you to
dream so big? Imagination, an open mind, lack of inhibition?

I believe we are born with an innate ability and tendency to
dream and imagine, and although I don't think that changes
as we grow older, *something* does. Something happens. But
what? What turns those dreams into fanciful illusions
instead of goals? And how do you get that optimism back?
Why have we accepted excuses as justifiable truths for not
achieving our goals, or for not even *pursuing* them, instead
of accepting the consequences to our choices—instead of
owning our lives? Somehow, we have let the beliefs of those
around us—and even our own beliefs and sense of self—
define the parameters of our success, the extent to which
we can realize our full potential. Unfortunately, that can be

quite limiting. Why do we let our dreams get clouded by a restricted version of 'reality', or by the *unlikelihood* of achieving a desired outcome? Are you sabotaging the possibilities of your life by focusing on the odds *against* achieving them?

ACCORDING TO *FORBES*, the odds of winning an Olympic gold medal are 1 in 662,000. That's more likely than being struck by lightning (1 in 2,300,000) but way less likely than winning an Oscar (1 in 11,500) or, say, being injured by a toilet (1 in 10,000).

If we looked only at the odds against us, or simply believed what we've always been told, what would actually be achieved in this world? What would be invented? What art would be created? What problems would be solved? Diseases cured? People saved?

To push myself to get to the top of the Olympic podium, I focused on the *possibilities* instead of the unlikelihood of my desired outcome—the 1 instead of the 662,000. To test what I was capable of and to challenge myself, I disregarded the odds. I crowded out the voice of experience (you know, the one that says, "You can't, how could you possibly, that's impossible or at least highly unlikely") to tap into my potential. Sure, I trained my body for the athletic feat, but I also trained my mind. To shift my perspective to dream big. To embrace challenges. To see if it was possible.

A FIVE-YEAR-OLD BOY had to have an operation to remove some skin that had become infected. It wasn't anything overly serious, but, as anyone would, when he awoke from the anaesthesia, he was thinking a lot about what had happened to him—how a small piece of him had been removed. He wasn't upset or crying—he's a pretty tough little kid—but obviously had a lot on his mind. A couple of days after the surgery, he very seriously and pensively asked his mother, "Does this mean I have to go to the other Olympics?"

"What do you mean?"

"The Olympics you go to if you're missing part of your body."

"Do you mean the Paralympics?

"Yes. Since part of my body was removed, do I have to go to those Olympics now?"

To that five-year-old boy, it was not a question of *whether* he would go to the Olympics and compete for his country on the international stage but simply *which one* he would be competing in. He wasn't thinking of the odds against. He wasn't thinking of the volumes of people who would be fighting for that same opportunity. He wasn't thinking of how others *might* be better than he is. He wasn't thinking of the repercussions of *not* achieving something he set out to accomplish. All he knew was that his Auntie had done it—had competed in the Olympics!—so it was clearly possibly. And there wasn't a single reason that crossed his mind as to why he, too, couldn't do the same thing. That little boy is my nephew.

To all my nieces and nephews, I am just 'Auntie', a 'normal' person who loves them and who also just happens to be an Olympic champion and internationally recognized rugby player. To my nieces and nephews, all under the age of eleven, what I accomplished in sports is just an ordinary possibility for *anyone* if they are willing to choose and follow that path, and put the work in, just like they could become a doctor like my sister if they wanted to heal the sick or a teacher like my brother if they preferred to help mould the minds of the next generation. To them, those outcomes are merely a matter of choice.

Some people might think this is a ridiculous statement, or that this line of thinking somehow diminishes my achievements on the international stage. I don't believe it does. I see it as the wide-eyed optimism of children that we need to encourage—the wide-eyed optimism that, unfortunately, too often gets diluted and fades with time and experience. It's the innocent, hopeful perspective that most adults have replaced with 'reality'—or at least a dampened and limiting version of what *they* have been led to believe is possible.

The Problem with 'Reality'

We squash so many dreams and goals in life with 'reality'. It starts when kids are little: *You can't do that, sweetie... Oh honey, you won't like that.* And it continues as adults: *Why on earth would you give up job security to pursue a pipe dream? Something with no guarantee?... You should be more realistic.*

But what *is* being 'realistic'? What exactly does it mean? People often justify this kind of 'reality check' by saying that it's better to put things in perspective for kids so they don't get their hopes up and, ultimately, get disappointed. Because,

Take a step toward the seemingly impossible, and you may start to see how possible it really is.

I mean ... what are the chances that the desired outcome will become a reality? 1 in 662,000, like the odds of winning an Olympic gold medal? Well, that's *something*! Chances are *zero* if they never try. Think about it this way: When your child is about to eat something you think they may not like, do you say something based on *your* experience to sway their opinion or do you let them try it first to find out for themselves whether they like it or not? The latter is about letting them discover and explore for themselves. The former is about projecting what *you* believe, and contaminating that experience for them—projecting *your* limiting beliefs of what is possible onto them.

Free to See the Possibilities

My trainer, Matt Nichol, once asked me why I thought I was so successful.

"What do you mean?" I responded.

"You've been successful in whatever you've truly set your mind to."

"I don't know about that ..."

"I'll tell you why. You said it to me a long time ago, and it is probably the key to your success just as much as, if not more than, any of your genetic gifts: It was that you grew up in a family where your parents never let you think that anything was impossible. You grew up assuming everything was possible, and believing that you could achieve what you set your mind to."

He was right. If you don't ever have that seed of doubt planted in your mind, you can truly find out what is possible because nothing (including society's interpretation of reality) will hold you back. My dreams changed constantly as a kid. I dreamed of becoming a photographer, a writer, a dancer, and, at one point, I was going to own my own zoo. My parents never shut me down. They never said, "Sunshine, let's think more *realistically*." They always responded with "What's the first thing you would do as a ... zoo-keeper? Or photographer?" Or "What are the steps you need to take to make it happen?" It was all about learning and growth, not rejecting possibility. And now, looking back, I realize they were, in fact, teaching me the techniques of goal-setting ... and *believing* in the possibilities. It was about setting a goal and simply (although not necessarily easily) finding a way.

What we believe to be possible or impossible is founded on what we experienced and were exposed to at a young age, which was then ingrained in our subconscious. Yes, experience can act as a building block to success—we learn through our experiences—but that learning can also introduce limiting beliefs, fear, and assumptions into your mind, preventing you from exploring the possibilities and discovering your capabilities. We need to take a step back and look at life's obstacles and opportunities through a wide-eyed, optimistic lens. Now, I'm not naively suggesting that *anything* is possible, but I *do* know that if you don't believe in the possibilities that *could* happen, you will definitely *not* achieve them. To be clear, there are definitely other factors beyond just belief in becoming successful, but you *won't* be successful if you don't actually believe that you can be.

A FRIEND AND mentor, and an author and leadership guru in his own right, John C. Maxwell once told a story about how he and his brother used to wrestle in their living room when they were growing up. His brother *always* used to pin him. One weekend, their father challenged John to a match. At first John thought that if he couldn't even beat his brother, how on earth was he going to beat his *father,* who was much bigger and stronger? But after some pretty serious effort, John pinned him. And, although nothing else had changed except for John's belief in his own abilities, the next time he wrestled his brother, he won.

How many other things are, in fact, possible but aren't pursued or even tested because of how *unlikely* the outcomes seem? Who do you know from your childhood who is doing something now because they defied the limiting assumptions that *you* had placed on the possibilities of that path? But I don't want you to focus on what could have been. I want that reflection to serve in moving you forward, focusing on the possibilities that exist in your present and in your future.

"The first step towards getting somewhere is to decide that you are not going to stay where you are!"

J.P. MORGAN

UNCOVER YOUR POTENTIAL

I T MAY SEEM to people who have heard me speak or who have followed my successes in sports that I have always embraced challenges and have always pushed my limits. But that is far from the truth. When I say that we are all capable of *way more* than we give ourselves credit for, I understand this from the other side more than most people realize. I know this from personal experience.

Yes, I have two Olympic gold medals. I have also competed internationally in track cycling *and* rugby, for which I was recently inducted into the World Rugby Hall of Fame. I worked as a Disability Sports Program Officer in Trinidad and Tobago, living there for almost three years, and completed a master's degree and certification in occupational therapy in 2007. But despite those accomplishments and despite how it might appear now, I was not always a driven, focused, goal-oriented, hard-working person or athlete. I wouldn't say I was lazy—I was a very active and involved child—but, for reasons I didn't realize at the time, I had lost my youthful optimism. I was unmotivated to push myself to improve, but, you see . . . at the time, I didn't really *have* to be.

That may sound arrogant, but it's not what you think. I'm not saying that I was the best and that I would always be the best. I just knew that I didn't *have* to work hard at performing at a level that would allow me to be selected and play on a team. At the time, my goal *wasn't* to be the best; it was simply to play. I just wanted to be part of a team and play. For fun. Because I enjoyed it.

I grew up in a town of fourteen thousand people, with only one high school. Without ever having to push myself too hard, I remained a top-tier competitor in the athletic community. I never took compliments well, but I have come to accept the fact that I am athletically gifted. But back in high school in a small community on Prince Edward Island, it had never occurred to me to push the limits, to discover the possibilities within my own innate potential. Hell, I didn't even see it!

Potential: Talent You Don't Have Yet

"Heather, you are the most frustrating athlete ever!"

That's not *exactly* what my high school coach said to me one day in his office. But, in hindsight, I can only imagine how frustrating I must have been to all my coaches.

As my high school's athletic banquet came to a close during my grade twelve (and final) year, Mr. Garth Turtle (the athletic director, gym teacher, and coach for a couple of the sports teams on which I played) called me into his office. Having come straight from the banquet room, I walked in with an armful of trophies and plaques, each emblazoned with some version of MVP, Most Talented Player, or Athlete of the Year. Mr. Turtle looked at me, took one of those deep breaths that are rooted in exasperation, and said, "Heather, you have *so* much potential..."

I half smiled because he was giving me a compliment and half-heartedly thanked him as I turned to leave, thinking that's all he wanted to say.

"But wait!" He stopped me in my tracks as I was reaching for the door. "I want you to understand that having *potential* means you really haven't accomplished anything yet, that all these trophies are nothing compared to what you could accomplish if you just tried. Potential is just talent that you *don't* have yet."

I'd like to say I understood the meaning of his words at that moment, and that I suddenly became focused and driven. But I can't. At the time, I probably just thought he was being weird. I only truly internalized his words and absorbed their meaning when I started bobsledding almost ten years later.

What I *did* understand then was that I was not getting the compliment I initially thought he was giving me. I was getting great advice . . . which I was in no way ready or willing to listen to yet.

The truth is, I knew I could be better, and so did Mr. Turtle. He hoped his 'compliment' would stoke a fire in me to put in more effort and try pushing myself: Stop being the naturally gifted social butterfly and taking my talents for granted. Stop wasting my athletic potential. I recently spoke with Mr. Turtle about that meeting. He said he remembers it vividly. He had been angry. Angry because still, to this day, he claims to have never seen an athlete (male or female) with as much athletic potential—potential being *wasted*. But, at the time, I wasn't concerned about my possibilities or how far I could go. Discovering what I was capable of wasn't my goal. I didn't *have* a goal. You see, up until then, I hadn't put much effort into my athletic performances—into really *working* for that armful of trophies. My mindset was not focused on potential. I was okay with being just good enough—and denying myself any chance of being great.

But What, Exactly, *Is* Potential?

According to the *Oxford Dictionary*, potential is the "capacity to become or develop into something in the future". Human potential is unrealized abilities—the possibilities of what one *could* achieve if a number of things were to happen (like hard work, skills development, opportunity, etc.). When something is said to be 'untapped', it means that it is underdeveloped or unused. An untapped keg means unused beer. And, although to many people that would be a tragedy, untapped *human* potential is, in my opinion, the biggest tragic waste of all. That's a complete shift in perspective from how I used to see things in school, and I have Mr. Turtle to thank, at least in part, for my shift in perspective. He saw in me what I couldn't, or wouldn't, see in myself. He saw the possibilities.

Are you doing just enough to get by? Or are you *thriving*?

Human potential is fascinating because everyone has a different amount of it in different areas of performance—athletically, academically, artistically, socially, emotionally, and so on. My father, for example, is brilliant in maths and sciences, while my mother is brilliant in languages and people skills. My mother's eyes glaze over at the thought of protons and algebraic equations, while my father's eyebrows raise questioningly at the sound of a foreign language. (He actually met my mother because she was tutoring him in French!)

Human potential is also fascinating because you only discover how much a person has when that potential is converted to skill or talent—when their innate ability is unlocked, or tapped into, to demonstrate a visible or apparent output in performance.

Through *Their* Lens

Potential is hidden inside all of us, but we don't know what kind of potential or how much—it has to be mined. It has to be discovered. Some people are able to recognize their own potential and tap into it (and this book aims to empower you to do just that). But often it takes someone or some*thing* else to be the catalyst, to help us become what we are truly capable of. Other people often see in us things we don't see in ourselves. Meaning: *They* see our potential. *They* see the possibilities that lie within our capacity. I have experienced that in sports but also in my speaking career. I have been fortunate to have developed mentorship relationships with a couple of very prominent speakers who, after watching me speak—hearing my message and seeing my ability to connect with people in my audiences—want to see me empower as many people as possible.

Sometimes you are aware of your strengths and the abilities you are currently able to demonstrate, but that's not the same as knowing your potential—what you could do or become, if you could only see the possibilities in yourself. The potential to be and do *way more* than you currently think you are capable of. Mr. Turtle was simply trying to unearth my potential—the talent I didn't have yet; he was trying to expose the possibilities that existed within my capacity. If only I had seen it then too…

Is Your Potential 'Gathering Dust'?

Too many people never fulfill their potential—never achieve what they are truly capable of. I was almost one of those people, which is why I've written this book. I have heard too many times that my athletic success was because I was athletically gifted. But had I not finally tapped into that athletic potential at the age of twenty-seven, it would have continued to be athletic potential 'gathering dust' while I pursued a mainstream and more 'realistic' career.

I had a strength—my explosive speed and power—that eventually transferred to a number of different sports on the international stage: rugby, bobsleigh, and track cycling. I don't need a medical test to know that I was born with more fast-twitch muscle fibres than the average person, and *that* was my potential. Potential is genetic. Speed and power, however, are talents and skills that must be developed from that potential—and that takes work. Many people are genetically predisposed with potential in specific areas, but too many of those people never convert their potential into talent, and never transform that talent into success. But ... *why not?*

Well, when did my *own* attitude change? What put a damper on *my* youthful optimism, causing me to be such a frustration to Mr. Turtle and my other coaches? What made it okay to be good enough—maybe better than others—but still not the best I could be? Why did I let myself downplay my abilities just to fit in?

Well, fast forward to years later, to the middle of a professional speakers workshop, examining certain subconscious beliefs and behaviours that were preventing us from becoming the best version of ourselves, as well as how they were developed. And it suddenly became very clear to me ...

"Look at Her"

It was in high school. I vividly remember the moment I decided to downplay my athletic abilities, even if I didn't realize it at the time. It was after overhearing a popular girl in my class quietly pointing out another classmate who was in the corner showing some dance move to her friend.

"Look at her. She thinks she's so much better than everyone else."

Subconsciously, I had internalized that comment. Although it hadn't been directed at me, it had still affected me to my core. *Do people think that of me because I'm good at sports? Would people think that of me if I showed the full extent of my abilities? If it seemed like I was trying to stand out from the crowd, would I be rejected like that?* People already might have thought I was better than they were at some things, but

I certainly didn't want anyone thinking that *I* thought I was better, or that I was *trying* to show anyone up. I also used to dance *and* sing (which I did outside of school, and kept somewhat separate from my school life because being good at *too* many things would just be too much). It would have been too much to excel in sports *and* music at school, so I didn't sing for the high school band. By then I knew what my coach knew: I had more natural athletic ability than most kids my age. I later discovered that that didn't only include kids on Prince Edward Island.

But instead of letting those talents come out, and working to improve and see how good I could become and how far I could go, I started to downplay everything. I didn't train—I didn't do anything extra outside of team practices. And even *in* those practices, I did only what was asked of me. Because I was still naturally athletic and generally the MVP on a lot of my teams, I made *sure* I wasn't also the coach's pet. I didn't show up early for practice. I didn't help set up equipment. I wasn't a team captain, and that was fine with me. Actually, *more* than fine. Because that *certainly* would have been too much!

> ## Are you only doing 100% of what is asked of you? Or 100% of what you are truly capable of?

Instead, I was the social person who drove my coaches crazy—because they saw the potential I was working so hard to ignore. To them, it was wasted. I tried to blend in as much as I could, or at least tried to appear like I didn't care so much. Make sure no one could say that I was *trying* to be better than they were. It's not that I didn't try and play hard in games. I did! I loved the competition, and I definitely played to win.

But I certainly wasn't a coach's dream at practice. They knew there was more inside me, but all they saw was a chatty girl half paying attention and keeping the extent of her talent buried.

I distanced myself from my achievements. No one could possibly think I was trying to make myself look better than anyone else or rubbing my accomplishments in anyone else's face. When I scored in soccer or rugby, I simply walked or jogged back to where I was supposed to be. No celebration. Just business. Because, without realizing it, I was too scared to stand out, for fear of being judged and being left out. I gradually developed the mindset that, by scoring or doing well, I was just doing my job—what I was *supposed* to do. Nothing worth celebrating. Not only was I downplaying my abilities externally but I also started downplaying them in my mind.

Hiding in Plain Sight

I'm not saying I was Supergirl, but, in a way, I learned what it feels like to conceal from the world what you are truly capable of. If I had had a dream of becoming an Olympic athlete when I was young, I might have acted differently. But that wasn't my dream at the time. I can't even say for sure what I would have done differently if that *had* been my dream. But my subconscious fears of judgment and rejection would most likely have stopped me before finding out what I could do— before discovering the extent of my athleticism and what I was truly capable of accomplishing. Even without giving it my full effort to become the best that I could be, deep down I knew what Mr. Turtle and my other coaches knew: I was capable of much more.

By the time I was a senior in high school, I actually contemplated quitting sports. I felt pressure from my coaches and my teammates, and I was starting to feel like the teams' outcomes depended on me. That may sound a bit overdramatic, but it's not. There were plays specifically designed to get the ball to me. And not just one or two! Normally I wouldn't have minded so much—I actually thrive under pressure—but for some reason I started to question my role on the teams. Did I even really *enjoy* sports anymore? Or was I just doing it because I was good at it? Or doing it out of a sense of obligation because of the *feeling* (whether there was any truth to it or not) that the teams' chances of winning would be reduced if I weren't part of the team? But, not being able to clearly define my feelings about the whole situation, and not wanting to make a rash decision and regret *not* playing, I just went with the flow and finished out my high school years playing on all those teams, earning Female Athlete of the Year (for the second year in a row).

Despite my lack of effort in practices, I was recruited for various universities in the Canadian Maritimes and also to an Ivy League school in the United States. But I wondered, Was I just being recruited because my name and reputation preceded me? Or was it because my older sister played varsity basketball? Or maybe my skills *were* good enough. But, regardless, I had that feeling of being pulled in different directions again, and, not being clear on what I truly wanted, I didn't know what to do. So I left.

I left Prince Edward Island—I actually left the Maritimes—and enrolled at the University of Waterloo in Ontario where I wasn't being recruited for a single thing or pressured to do anything. Why? Because nobody there knew who I was or knew anything about my athletic history or abilities. I chose that university because it offered the academic science-based kinesiology program I wanted, and also because it had a track team with a very reputable national track coach.

I thought it would be interesting to see what I could do with some technical coaching. But never having visited the university campus before, I hadn't realized until I showed up that the university didn't even have a track!

In the summer between my second and third year at university, the boyfriend of one of my soccer teammates (I played soccer in the fall semesters before doing track in the winter semesters) asked me if I would join a local club rugby team to play in a tournament that weekend because the team was short on numbers. I told him that I hadn't played in over two years but wouldn't mind filling in if they really needed someone. The first time I got my hands on the ball and ran almost the full length of the field to score a try, I knew that I wouldn't be going back to soccer. Not because I scored but because of the thrill of running with the ball in my hands and the sense of community within the sport. I hadn't realized how much I had missed playing rugby. That night, before the rugby tournament was even over, I called my soccer coach and explained how I was feeling. I loved the girls on my team, had so much respect for my coach, and had sincerely enjoyed my time with them, but I *loved* rugby. I was finally becoming more self-aware. Or, at least, was more willing to listen to what my heart was telling me, and make conscious decisions that were right for *me*.

Mr. Turtle had seen the raw material inside me—the athletic potential I was lucky to have been born with—and he had wanted me to turn it into talent. The talent I 'didn't *have* yet'. He knew I was capable of *way more*; I just wasn't ready to hear it at the time. And, because of that, I had been stifling my potential.

"You may be better than the rest, but you are not a success until you have made the effort to become the best you can be."

COACH JOHN WOODEN

THINK OF IT this way: Potential is like the Genie in the bottle. He is contained inside the tiny lamp until somebody rubs it to release him—to release the potential that three requests can bring. Some people rub the lamp simply to clean it—working away without realizing the consequences of where that work could take them. Others need someone else to *tell* them to rub the lamp—tell them if they were only to put in some effort, their potential could be revealed. And some people will seek out the lamp and rub it vigorously just to *see* what kind of potential might lie within it, having a goal that only truly tapping into their potential will help them achieve.

Well, you know which group *I* fit into in high school. Now, I'm not saying that any one of these three groups is better than the others. I'm simply saying it's important to be aware and vigilant. Be aware of what others are indicating about your abilities, listen to what they are saying about your strengths, and be open to explore opportunities that you may never have considered before. And be a person who reveals the potential of *others*. Be a promoter—an advocate—of human achievement, success, and the discovery and fulfillment of potential. Of human possibility.

To successfully convert raw material—potential—into talent, it takes a lot of hard work and self-belief. Some people believe that a supportive environment is critical to thrive. Although it helps (and it certainly helped me), there are many inspiring stories of people who have achieved success despite their background, challenging circumstances, and lack of support. Every time I see a plant growing through a crack in the sidewalk or on a brick wall, I'm reminded of the resiliency and determination of people. It's time to stop dwelling on the things you don't have and focus on the things you *do* have— your strengths, the things that are in your favour, the things that are in your control. The pursuit of personal excellence comes down to a choice.

> **The possibilities for your future lie within the degree to which you take the steps toward realizing your potential.**

Believe in the Possibilities

Belief is a powerful thing, and is the first—and most important—step in achieving a goal or overcoming an obstacle or a setback (which can be a goal in and of itself). I am referring to the belief that achieving that goal is a *possibility* and, therefore, is worthy and justified in pursuing.

For some, believing in possibilities requires a shift in perspective—a paradigm shift, as it is referred to in business—which is essential to take things to the next level, to make some fundamental behavioural changes, and to achieve their highest level of performance and success (which we'll examine in more detail in the next chapter). Whether you see the possibilities first, or it takes someone else to point them out to you, it's critical to *believe* in them to make them happen. As we'll explore later in the book, obstacles will get in your way, but your belief in the possibilities will give you the determination and motivation to follow the path you choose.

Sometimes it is the people closest to you who first see your potential and maintain a steadfast belief in your abilities and possibilities. For me, it's my family, and this book is filled with stories of my childhood—lessons my siblings and I learned from my parents. I feel very fortunate to have an amazingly supportive family—a family who doesn't really emphasize what I've accomplished as long as I have kept my integrity and compassion for others. Don't get me wrong—they are extremely proud of me for what I've accomplished in my life so far, but they are more proud of the person I am. Growing up, my parents didn't put much weight on their children's accomplishments but rather on our character—our effort and how we treated others. My parents are just as proud of my sister and my brother as they are of me, because they, too, have been able to make a living doing something they love while helping other people. And I am equally as proud of my siblings and my parents for what *they* stand for, the integrity by which they all live their lives, and the examples they set.

I am extremely fortunate to have a very close family, and for the longest time, I thought everyone had. But I have come to realize that the family I have is, unfortunately, very rare. Not everyone has the benefit of having a truly supportive family. Not everyone has the benefit of growing up having the permission to dream big, feeling safe to question assumptions and take risks, and learning to think about, and believe in, the possibilities.

Although you may not have had the benefit of growing up in a family like mine, or of having those positive beliefs ingrained in you as a young child, you can cultivate your own. Support systems come in very different forms and descriptions. You can decide who deserves to be part of your inner circle—*your* support family.

And don't forget: *I*, too, believe in you! Which is the reason I wrote this book. I *truly* believe that you are capable of *way more* than you are giving yourself credit for right now. And I am excited for the possibilities of your life. I am excited for the moment when *you* start believing in those possibilities too. Because until then, you are selling yourself short.

For some, this book may simply be an interesting read—insight into the life of an elite athlete, from small town to the top of the Olympic podium. But it may also act as a catalyst, a mentor, a friendly reminder, a shift in perspective, a trigger, a kick in the pants, a get-your-ass-in-gear pep talk, or simply a source of inspiration and motivation—the boost you need to embrace the challenge and the journey to extraordinary achievement and fulfillment. To believe in the possibilities that exist in whatever circumstance you find yourself in. To move from excuses to potential. To discover what you are *truly* capable of.

3

ADJUST YOUR FOCUS

GREW UP ON Prince Edward Island (affectionately called P.E.I. by all Islanders and most Canadians). The smallest Canadian province, at approximately 4,800 square kilometres, is nestled off the east coast in the Atlantic Ocean and is home to fewer than 145,000 people. No matter where I travel or how long I am away, I will always call P.E.I. 'home'. My parents still live in Summerside in the same house they moved into with my older sister and me when I was only three weeks old.

People have described P.E.I. as enchanted, a hidden secret, and it is! Every time I return home, at the first glimpse of 'my' Island, I feel at peace; a sense of calm comes over me as I inhale that first breath of fresh salt air that comes from being on a small island cradled in the ocean. The landscape is postcard-perfect at almost every turn, full of the storybook settings that Lucy Maud Montgomery captured in her book *Anne of Green Gables*. Many have described this landscape from the air as looking like a patchwork quilt, with rows of green trees or red roads separating the various 'quilt squares' of vibrant yellow canola fields, golden hay fields, light green corn fields, bright green ribbons of vegetation, and fields that look like corduroy in the spring—the endless rows of potato fields with their green tops sprouting through the raised rows of bright red dirt. That's right! I said *red*! It's red because of the iron oxide in the soil. P.E.I. is not an island of rock—it is, in fact, an island of sandstone. And although that poses its own problems—like potholes in our roads every spring because of the shifting ground throughout the winter (and I wouldn't necessarily recommend March or April as the best months to visit for the first time)—it is my home and it is beautiful!

The "Come from Away" Lens

Come from away is a colloquial phrase used by Prince Edward Islanders (although I've recently heard that it's also used by people from other islands and small towns) to refer to anyone who lives on the Island but was not born there. These people are often referred to as CFAs for short. (In fact, this phrase has recently become much more familiar to many people thanks to the Tony-Award-winning Broadway musical *Come From Away*—a Canadian play set in the Atlantic provinces, specifically Newfoundland and Labrador.)

According to this definition, both of my parents are CFAs. My mother grew up in Montreal and only moved to the Island in 1972 after marrying my father. And although most Islanders would dispute my father's status because his family was established on the Island for at least five generations before him, he is technically a CFA because he was born in Halifax (which was much better equipped in those days to safely manage the delivery of my grandmother's high-risk pregnancy).

I would *never* be considered a CFA to Islanders, though. And I am as proud an Islander as they come—the purest definition of 'you can take the girl out of the Island, but you can't take the Island out of the girl'. However, I have been fortunate to have travelled a lot and have lived in many different places. A lot of what I've accomplished has been, technically, as a CFA—'from away'—meaning that I did it somewhere *other* than where I'm from—somewhere *away* from my comfort zone of home.

And that has afforded me the opportunity to see my home, my life, and myself from a different perspective. Everyone's point of view and sense of self are shaped by their surroundings. For some, this can become very limiting. The problem with seeing things from only one perspective is that you may not see the possibilities that lie beyond the limitations of that point of view. CFAs may be different, and may even appear threatening to some because they are different, but they also may open your eyes to see things in a new way because they come from a different place, have experienced different things, have faced different challenges, have met different people, and have made or witnessed different choices followed by an array of consequences.

Our perspective is shaped by our surroundings, which includes our personal geography, that is, all the influences that directly impact our lives—mentally, physically, and/or emotionally. The downside to that personal geography being too comfortable, however, is that you never want to leave. And sometimes being too comfortable doesn't allow you to discover your potential and see what's possible. Sometimes you have to 'go away', outside of your comfort zone, to see the potential in a situation or in yourself.

The ability to shift perspective is a good thing. It allows you to see new or old opportunities in a different way, and to see seemingly insurmountable problems or setbacks in another light, often helping to reveal possible solutions that otherwise wouldn't have been obvious. Just like when someone turns on a light, you see more of whatever it was you were trying to look at in the dark. It's a lot easier to see the details of a particular situation! For some, leaving their comfort zone could mean moving to a new town, starting a new job, giving birth to your first child (or second). For me, leaving P.E.I. was a catalyst to see myself, my potential, and my life in a different way—*coming from away*.

The perspective that *others* can give you is a *come from away* perspective—a view from outside yourself that lets you see yourself or a situation with fresh eyes. I'm not saying that you should always adopt other people's perspective, or that you should automatically ditch your original goal if another offer comes along. But sometimes it's not an opportunity that comes up, but rather another person and the perspectives that *they* possess, that can be a catalyst in your life for

The problem
with seeing things
from only one
perspective is that
you may not see
the possibilities
that lie beyond the
limitations of that
point of view.

releasing your hidden potential—potential that you may not have even realized you had. So be open to hearing what others have to say, how they speak of your strengths.

Walk in Someone Else's Shoes

When was the last time you heard the phrase *walk in someone else's shoes*? Have you ever stopped to consider what it means? What it *really* means? What it means to *you*? It's a phrase that is usually intended to induce empathy for someone else's situation. Being able to *walk in someone else's shoes* means putting yourself in their position, seeing a particular situation from *their* point of view, having walked a different path in life, with different past experiences, beliefs, and outlooks as the lens through which *they* would interpret that very same situation, in turn giving you a different perspective.

It means seeing problems or setbacks from the other person's perspective, but also seeing solutions from their point of view. That is the benefit of the *come from away* perspective shift: seeing situations from another point of view and discovering otherwise unseen solutions that will broaden your outlook and help you tap into your own potential. So... walk in someone else's shoes. Imagine *their* experiences and how *they* would interpret a situation. Imagine the solutions *they* could see within your circumstance. Do you have a strong opinion about something? Can you see how someone else might be able to justify a different opinion about that very same thing? And can you understand how *they* might have come to have that opinion? Just as you would walk in someone else's shoes to understand them better, it's important to see your own life, or simply your current situation, in a fresh, new way to discover the potential that waits deep within you.

The Beach Ball Method

Adopting a different perspective can also be helpful in overcoming the obstacles that will inevitably present themselves en route to achieving your goals. You must be able to step back and come at the perceived problem *from away*. This allows you to see potential solutions that you would most likely not have seen otherwise. Imagine a typical beach ball. If you and a group of people are sitting in a circle with the beach ball in the middle, when looking at it from any one position, each person can see only three of the coloured sections on the ball at any one time, no matter where each person is sitting. However, if you *come from away* and switch seats with someone else to see the ball from another perspective, you will be able to see three different coloured sections of the ball.

Imagine if the solution to your problem was written on one of the sections that you couldn't see from your original vantage point! You may have even been close to the solution—only one section away—but without a slight shift in perspective, you would not have been able to see it. This goes to show that being able to step back and see problems or setbacks from a different point of view—to *come from away*—is often crucially important to overcoming obstacles, achieving your goals, and, ultimately, reaching your highest level of success.

Come from away is a metaphor for coming at any problem from a different perspective—whether you're able to make that shift yourself or via a catalyst (whether a pivotal moment or another person)—which makes you see things that will, in turn, enable you to continue moving toward your goal.

"The world as we have created it is a process of our thinking. It cannot be changed without changing our thinking."

ALBERT EINSTEIN

Unlike Most Olympians...

I've already told you that I did *not* grow up dreaming about competing in the Olympics. I did not grow up on P.E.I. with people around me training to represent their country. To me, Olympians were 'TV people'—not everyday, normal people like I considered myself to be. Historically, there had only been eleven Olympians from all of P.E.I. *Ever!* None of them had come from my small town, and they were so few and far between across the Island anyway that I just don't think it really registered for me that a future career in sports was a practical or possible pursuit.

Nor did my very academically oriented family really prioritize sports. We didn't even watch many sports on TV besides the occasional playoff game (for which I would choose a team to cheer for based on the colours or logos on their uniforms) or specific highly anticipated Olympics events (for which I would obviously cheer for Canada if we were in it). Sure, I played sports (as did my brother and sister), and lots of them, but just for fun. I always considered sports to be something extracurricular to what I was going to do to earn a living. I did not start training for sports—taking it seriously or even lifting weights—until I was twenty-seven years old, when I was suddenly faced with the challenge of seeing if I could learn a new sport, learn to do it well, and learn to do it well enough to qualify and compete in the Olympics only five months later!

Not knowing anything about the sport of bobsledding (besides what I'd seen in the movie *Cool Runnings* years prior), I agreed to take part in the recruitment testing camp for the Canadian National Bobsleigh Team at the end of August 2005, leading up to the 2006 Olympics in Turin (Torino), Italy (more on how this came about below). However, I had no intention of actually *competing*. Someone *else* saw the potential in me. And although that, in and of itself, didn't help change my perspective of the possibilities, being open to the opportunity and going to the tryouts provided the pivotal moment that *did* change my perspective—the moment that made me suddenly see things in a whole new way. I saw the possibilities *from away*. I stepped out of 'high school' and immediately saw a different section of the beach ball.

At that testing camp at Calgary's Canada Olympic Park, I broke one of the team's national testing records (for the timed, weighted sled-pull test)! And a tryout that started as a way to appease the recruiter who had first tried, and failed, to recruit me before the 2002 Salt Lake City Olympics suddenly turned into a pivotal moment—a challenge that I couldn't seem to resist because I suddenly saw this opportunity from a different perspective: Could I really represent my country in the Olympics five months later in a sport I'd never done before? Was it possible?

Was it likely that someone with my background, who had never trained seriously before, who had less than five months to learn an unfamiliar sport at the age of twenty-seven, would eventually make it to the Olympics three times and win two gold medals? No. At least not from my perspective of needing to downplay my abilities. Not until I was able to look at my own life and its possibilities *from away*.

Highly unlikely! But apparently, in hindsight, still very much *possible*!

MY ACHIEVEMENTS IN sports would never have been a possibility—even a thought in my brain—if someone had not seen potential in me ... and had I not agreed (at least the second time!) to be open to new experiences and opportunities.

You see, in June 2001, I had just returned to P.E.I. for the summer after working in Ireland for five months and was having dinner with my parents when the phone rang. It was Dennis Barrett, the track coach from McGill University in Montreal. I had competed against Dennis's athletes when I sprinted for the University of Waterloo in my undergraduate years and had gotten to know Dennis a bit at some joint training camps over the Christmas breaks. During that phone call, Dennis told me that he had recently been asked by Bobsleigh Canada to do some recruiting in Eastern Canada. Apparently, he had competed in the sport before, and would know what to look for. He had seen me run and thought that as a power sprinter I had the ideal combination of strength and speed to be a good bobsleigh brakeman. He wanted me to come to the testing for the 2002 Salt Lake City Olympics, which, at the time, were less than a year away. I told him I wasn't interested. He told me I could be an Olympian. I quietly laughed and said, "No, thank you. I'm just not interested."

I didn't really give bobsledding any serious consideration because I had already accepted an internship to work in Trinidad and Tobago as a Disability Sports Program Officer, and

I had always wanted (at least since my late teens) to work in a developing country—*not* to compete in the Olympics! Especially in the sport of bobsleigh, about which I knew nothing. So I turned Dennis down and ended up working in Trinidad for almost three years until I moved back to Canada to pursue my master's degree in occupational therapy.

One year into my master's, and almost exactly four years after that first phone call, I ran into Dennis at my former track coach's retirement party. "I know you're older now, and I know it would be more difficult," he stated, "but I saw that you ran a couple of races this year, and that you're still fast. I still think you should do this." Dennis is nothing if not persistent. I finally relented. After all, taking part in a testing camp didn't commit me to anything, and it wasn't going to stop me from continuing my education. It was only going to be for a week. And in the big scheme of things, what's a week?

I did the testing without ever having touched a bobsled or even having seen one in real life. And when I broke at least one of the testing records at the tryout, I was shocked. Dennis had told me that I would do well, but I had no frame of reference to believe that I could compete with athletes at that level. I then started to wonder if I *could* actually do it. Could I learn a new sport well enough to qualify and compete in the Torino Olympics? And could I do it in less than five months?

It was then when I realized I am motivated and fuelled by challenges. Why had I not realized that before? Because, having grown up in a small town, competing in sports had come naturally to me and therefore had been unchallenging at that level. In P.E.I., I had not been exposed to other levels for which to strive. I also hadn't been challenged academically—not because I was some kind of genius but because at the time I hadn't known what career I wanted to pursue. I had

had no direction—no purpose—so my only goal, really, had been to graduate and move on to university where, perhaps, I would discover a purpose, a passion.

But to try to do something that most people would think implausible? There were definitely no guarantees, and qualifying for the Olympics in such a short time was highly unlikely, but . . . it fuelled me. It wasn't about the guarantees. It wasn't about the Olympics. It was about the challenge. It was about seeing how close I could get.

I embraced the challenge. I didn't consider it a life-altering decision at the time—it was about realizing that I could press the pause button on certain pursuits to try other ones. That I really *could* give it a shot. That it was a choice. And that it was only five months of my life to try something new and see what I could do within that time. It was about realizing I didn't *have* to finish my master's degree in two years. I redefined the rules—the parameters that were guiding how I was living my life. I gave myself permission to live a new adventure, and see if I could uncover the potential that others saw in me. So I flew back to Toronto and with the help of my faculty advisor applied for a one-year leave of absence from my master's program.

Putting my studies on hold for a year wasn't an easy decision until I got out of my own way by asking myself if I could meet the challenge of an unexpected opportunity and by questioning my assumptions of what I believed I was *supposed* to do, how I was *supposed* to live. I knew that if I had not made the choice to go for it, I could have become a very happy occupational therapist. What would be wrong with that? Nothing! I *love* occupational therapy. But without making that choice and taking that chance, I would never have known that I was capable of *much* more than I ever dreamed possible or of being able to positively impact more people than I ever could have imagined. I would never have known that I could push myself to a completely different place from where my preconceived expectations of my life had led me.

I simply want you, like me, to accept the people and things in your life that *come from away*—that allow you to see things from another perspective. Learn to be aware of the opportunities that exist—learn to recognize them, and assess whether they are right for you and aligned with your priorities—and then recognize that your path is a choice. You get to choose your goals. And the more you can acknowledge all the opportunities along the way (and the possibilities that exist within those opportunities), and intentionally choose your goals, the happier you will be with your choices and your outcomes because you will have pursued something by choice instead of by default.

BOBSLEIGH 101: BRAKING

There is an opening at the bottom of the sled through which the brakes descend to scrape and grab hold of the ice. This happens by the brakeman pulling up and back on handles that are lying almost flat along the bottom of the sled. When this action is implemented, the steel comb-like brakes descend through the opening. Since brakemen often have to slow a sled going 140 to 150 km/hr down to zero in a very short distance, braking stretches are often on an incline so that gravity can help. (Note: Some people get caught up on the term *brakeman*, thinking that it should be *brakewoman*. But I simply think of it in terms of mankind. Humankind.)

WHEN I MADE the choice to try bobsledding, I started doing things I had never done before, like training and lifting weights, because if I was going to take on this challenge I wanted no regrets about the result. Now, I had missed the first day of testing because it overlapped with the Canadian Rugby Championships. Because it had been a previous commitment, the bobsleigh development coach approved my absence on the first day. Which was very fortunate for me because that first day of testing just happened to be all strength testing. Weights! And I had never lifted weights before! Because I am naturally muscular and physically strong, I think people had always just assumed I worked out and lifted weights, which is probably one reason why I never did. I mean, if I already looked like I lifted weights, what would I look like if I really *did*?

I can only envision two outcomes had I been in attendance that first day. I can't imagine me revealing to anyone at a national testing camp that I had never lifted weights before, so I probably would have either embarrassed myself or injured myself trying to copy other people's technique. But realistically?... Probably both!

But if I joined the bobsleigh team for the World Cup circuit, I wasn't sure how I could continue to get away with *not* lifting weights anymore...

I called my sister and asked what I should do: "I'm going to be on tour with the other athletes on the team. How will I be able to get away with not lifting weights?"

I'd like to say there was a pause on the phone while she actually contemplated my concern and serious question, but there wasn't. "Get over yourself," she said (in a way that only a close sister or best friend can get away with). "Just lift weights! It's only five months of your life, and you're not going to want to look back and wonder what *could* have happened if you'd only done it. Imagine how you would feel if you *just* missed qualifying for the Olympics because you refused to lift weights!"

She was right. (Don't tell her I said that.) That one statement helped me shift my perspective. I didn't want any regrets. I didn't want to look back on my life and wonder "What if?" And, for the first time, I *actively* started pursing a big goal.

So, I invite you to shift your perspective and be fuelled by challenges like I am. Open yourself to the possibilities that others see in you. Or open yourself up to the possibilities that exist beyond the limitations you have set for yourself; to discover what you're capable of beyond the limits of what you have deemed to be 'practical' or 'realistic' goals. You never know what exists beyond your self-limiting beliefs and the same old comfortable routine of life. Give yourself permission to try something new and different, or try something in a new way. Give yourself permission to question what you have always believed to be true, set goals beyond your comfort zone and beyond what you currently believe to be possible, and head toward realizing your full potential.

By facing our challenges, we discover our potential.

ANONYMOUS

PART

2

SEIZE

YOUR

POTENTIAL

4

WHAT'S STOPPING YOU?

DO YOU EVER feel like the deck is stacked against you? You think you're too fat or too thin. You bombed a big presentation and lost a client. Your roof is leaking. You just got dumped. Your kid is failing at school. You hate your job. You got a flat tire on your way to an important meeting. You never seem to have time to spend with your family. No matter how strong you are in your belief, or how goal-oriented you are, there will always be obstacles to achieving the life you want—things that are standing between where you are and the finish line you want to reach. No time. No money. No support.

When talking about goals that weren't achieved (or even pursued), people often talk about the obstacles that stood in their way to achieving their desired outcome or prevented them from realizing their full potential. These deterrents can include finances, careers, family circumstances, internal politics, resources, in-laws, physical abilities or injuries, and time, and they are often referred to as *external* obstacles. Of course, achieving success would be easier if all these things worked in our favour, but even people born with the prover-bial silver spoon in their mouth sometimes *never* achieve anything or *never* feel a real sense of fulfillment. And often people who have come from the worst circumstances you can imagine reach the epitome of success, becoming someone we, as society, tend to admire. So why do some people allow obsta-cles to block their intentions and ambitions, while others seem to easily overcome any roadblock that life throws in their way? Why and how do some people reach their potential in spite of life's hurdles, while others remain defeated by them?

Obstacles are only obstacles if you perceive them to be, and they will stop you from moving forward only if you let them. This book will help you realize it's all a matter of perspective. Perspective has everything to do with whether you see an obstacle preventing you from achieving your goal, or a chal-lenge providing you with the opportunity to see how creative, innovative, and/or determined you can be to overcome it. In this chapter, we'll examine in detail a few of the more com-mon external factors that often stand in the way of our goals.

"If you can find a path with no obstacles, it probably doesn't lead anywhere."

FRANK A. CLARK

Physical Limitations

Physical limitations—either a disability you are born with or an injury that either temporarily or permanently results in a deficit in physical function—are an obstacle to achieving your dreams. But, again, it is a matter of perspective. Helen Keller was born deaf *and* blind but earned a bachelor of arts degree and became an activist. Bethany Hamilton, a professional surfer, barely survived a shark attack in 2003. Although she lost her left arm, she returned to competition and became known as one of the best female surfers in the world. And there are countless amputees who have climbed various mountains around the world, including Everest and the Matterhorn. These people all may seem like rare, extreme cases of determination, but they show what is possible if you focus on the goal and not the limitations. These kinds of stories are more common than you may think. Check out YouTube to see people like Mark Goffeney, born without arms, play the guitar beautifully with his feet!

As an athlete, I have had my share of injuries, and I always just considered to them to be setbacks—not deal-breakers. But dealing with physical issues started well before I was introduced to sports. I was born with one of my feet twisted and for the first few months of my life had to wear special shoes with a bar attaching them together to keep my foot straight.

Growing up, I was always an extremely fast sprinter, but I had a funny way of running. My knees kind of kicked out to the sides, and I pushed off the ground in an externally rotated gait. My track coach at university, after seeing me sprint for the first time, said, "I have no idea how you run so fast, running the way you do. Why didn't anyone ever tell you to lift your knees?"

Well, I *tried* to lift my knees while sprinting. I knew that a higher knee lift would ultimately result in a greater downward force output, making me faster. What I didn't know for all those years, but was revealed in a magnetic resonance imaging (MRI) in 2012, was that my hip sockets were rotated, angling slightly backwards. This may or may not have been connected to the twisted foot I had been born with, but it was then that I realized whatever I had accomplished up until that point, I had done so *despite* my hip flexion being restricted by bone—that there had been a *reason* for me not being able to lift my knees higher. Either way, although my impediments could have been an obstacle to achieving my goals, I chose to see them as challenges.

"Genetically influenced doesn't mean genetically determined."

SCOTT BARRY KAUFFMAN

Technology

How far away from you is your phone right now? When is the last time you glanced at its screen? When's the last time you received a notification? A ding? A ring? A buzz?

When I was growing up, there weren't cell phones in the pockets of eight- and nine-year-olds. There weren't even cell phones in the pockets of adults, for that matter. From what I knew, cell phones were in trunks. Let me explain... Cell phones are a fairly recent invention and weren't in wide-spread use when I was a young girl. By the time I was in high school, there *were* cell phones, but they were still rare devices the size of bricks and were found in the trunks of some vehicles, to be used only in emergencies. My grandparents had one of those, and at the time, my siblings and I thought it was a bit excessive (although kinda cool and obviously smart if you had an emergency). The phone was turned on only to make outgoing calls—to call the police in case of an accident or a tow truck if you needed roadside assistance. Nobody had the number because there was no point. If they called it, the phone would have been turned off. And even if it *had* been turned on, the ringer would have been hard to hear, since the phone was in a case in the trunk.

Times *have* changed. And, for the most part, the changes have *added* to our lives. But often when something is added, something else is taken away. Technology has evolved so quickly that I don't think we have learned to adjust effectively or in a healthy way to all those changes.

We are now living in a time when we are constantly con-nected—inundated with information and requests at every turn. Yes, with technology comes efficiency. But instead of technology opening up more time for us to do the things we are truly passionate about, we are faced with heightened expectations about how readily available we should be at all times, how quickly we should respond, and how much we can accomplish. Because it's possible to be connected 24/7 and tasks can be done in less time than before, others expect that we can (and will) get *more* things done in that same amount of time.

This frenetic pace is having an impact on our health and wellness. Take a few minutes to consider the following questions: Do you not have time for that personal project or goal because your boss or your clients expect you to respond immediately and at all hours of the day or night? Can't get to even *formulating* your own goals because you just have to keep up on social media? Or, honestly, are you using your reliance on technology and the busy-ness it encourages as a justification *not* to pursue your full potential?

Yes, technology can be an incredibly powerful tool you can leverage to help you achieve your goals and chart your progress. However, for several reasons, technology is a definite obstacle to achieving your goals. It impacts your productivity as a major source of distraction, always at your immediate disposal. It affects your mental health as the heightened expectations can lead to stress and anxiety, not to mention a pace that cannot physically be maintained forever. And the constant connectedness to the world, being bombarded with the priorities and urgencies of others, influences your ability to really connect with yourself in a way that helps you identify and fully understand not only what is important to *you* and what you truly *want* but also the *potential* within you.

Disconnect to Reconnect

It is becoming increasingly important to disconnect—to unplug from distractions and the causes of your stress and anxiety. I'm not just talking about turning off your Wi-Fi and phone ringer to be more productive in your day. I'm advising to create physical, emotional, and mental spaces that allow you to truly disconnect in order to reconnect to yourself, taking the time to tap into your thoughts, feelings, and potential. Time away from your daily pressures, stresses, routines, and responsibilities allows for the uninterrupted opportunity to tap into your values, re-evaluate your priorities, and help make life choices that are right for you.

AS A SELF-EMPLOYED physician, my father didn't get paid for sick days or holidays. But it was important to him to always take the month of August off to be with the family at the cottage. Now, having since been to a number of different types of cottages, I must clarify that our family cottage was (and still is, for the most part) quite rustic—a cabin in the woods right by the water, no manicured lawn (actually, *no* lawn, just woods), no insulation, a community party-line for the phone (although the number was not listed, and was only known by a few relatives and a neighbour in town in case of an emergency), no television (just a radio for occasional weather reports), a shower with extremely limited hot water... you get the picture.

When I was a kid, we didn't have the Internet, smartphones, tablets, or any other media devices, especially at the cottage. There were no outside distractions. Only time. Time to actually *be* with each other. Time to just *be* with ourselves. Time to just... *be*. We had no choice but to be in the present moment. Entertainment was swimming or canoeing, watching the birds, hand-feeding the chipmunks, playing card games, reading, collecting starfish, catching crayfish, watching the water, watching the wind in the leaves of the trees...

You may be wondering why I'm sharing this story. Well, I'm often asked how I could handle being involved in so many things as a child. In reflecting on my childhood, wondering how, in fact, I *was* able to take part in so many activities, I realized that it had to do with the opportunity to recharge my batteries. As I discuss in more detail later in the book, our household had a Family Day rule: one mandatory day a week (Sunday) to relax together (having done homework and chores the day before). In hindsight, those Sundays recharged me enough to handle whatever was thrown at me during the week. But a full month of being disconnected? And, in turn, being *connected* to myself, to my family, and to the present moment? Essential.

In today's chaos of life, we forget what benefits we get from doing nothing. But I believe that most people have forgotten *how* to disconnect to take advantage of those benefits. So much focus and productivity is lost because of our inability to disconnect, because of our misguided beliefs that being busy is equivalent to being productive and that public success and recognition are the same things as happiness and fulfillment.

Our choices become easier to make when we are in tune with our priorities, which, in turn, comes from being in tune with ourselves. And we are dynamic beings that are ever-changing and evolving. Therefore, our priorities may be changing too. We must give ourselves the opportunity to disconnect—to recharge *and* reconnect with ourselves—because it's not about being busy and getting recognition but living a productive and fulfilled life.

You may not have a cabin in the woods to go to, but you can find your version of it. A retreat, a few nights at a hotel (even if it's just down the street), even a room in your house or a park around the corner. No matter the location, just make the time to disconnect, to unplug by stepping away from not only the technological demands and distractions but also the multitude of things that impact us in a negative way—the noise, the things that pull us in so many different directions (both physically and emotionally), all contributing to our chronic stress and anxiety and, ultimately, our lack of focus, productivity, fulfillment, and success. No wonder it's so challenging for people to discover their potential, let alone achieve it. In our modern world, less could really be ... *more*.

Some *People!*

Unless you live alone in a cabin in the woods (which might actually sound quite appealing based on what we just discussed about technology), people are very much a part of your environment. As mentioned, people can be catalysts who help you recognize your potential in the first place or can serve as an incredible support group as you strive for your goals; unfortunately, some can become obstacles on that path, limiting how far you go rather than lifting you up. Again, and I think you may be getting the picture by now, it depends on perspective—not only how the people around us see the world and interact with us but also who you choose to surround yourself with. There are all kinds of people in the world. It is important to align yourself with the ones who will support you in striving to be your best, not the ones who will drag you down.

There are some people who suck the energy right out of you. Energy-takers are the glass-half-empty people—those who not only see problems but also how things could get worse, complaining all the time to ensure that everyone else sees the problems too. These energy-takers may present in different ways, but the result is always the same: bringing others down. They constantly seem to be pointing out the negative side of things, distrusting everything and everyone, complaining about everything and everyone because nothing or no one is ever good enough, always passing the blame and never taking ownership of their actions, always making themselves out to be the victims, having been wronged by... well, everything and everyone!

You know who I'm talking about. You feel an extreme sense of gratitude when conversations with these people are interrupted and cut short because you weren't sure how much more of it you could have taken.

Energy-takers are toxic to productivity and are obstacles to achieving your full potential because they make you question your own beliefs of what is possible. They may even be trying to help by suggesting that you be more 'realistic' in your goals!

There are two distinct kinds of energy-takers: lobsters (or those suffering from what is called "lobster syndrome") and naysayers. And both can be just as detrimental to you achieving your goals, whether they are personal or group/ team goals. Let me explain.

Energy-Taker #1: Lobsters

Atlantic lobster is internationally associated with P.E.I., as are mussels and potatoes—all big industries for the little island on which I grew up. P.E.I. lobster season is something that Islanders look forward to and visitors often plan their holidays around, ensuring at least one lobster feast during their stay. My sister, for example, now lives in Denver, but she and her family visit for a couple of weeks every summer. There is a lobster dinner 'quota' that has to be filled while she is there, to tide her over until she returns again the next summer—a tradition that I am definitely not averse to helping her maintain.

As delicious as lobsters are, their behaviour when trapped in a bucket or aquarium is not at all appealing. If you ever watch lobsters in a tank, you may notice that, regardless of how shallow the tank, the lobsters don't escape. Why not? Because any time a lobster tries to climb out, the others pull it back down into the water. This is, unfortunately, symbolic of society. People like to see others do well . . . to an extent. And then people who suffer from lobster syndrome (also sometimes referred to as *crab mentality* or *crabs in a bucket*) end up trying to pull them back down, intimidated by the person who is genuinely trying to better his or her circumstances. We often see this in movies about gangs or ghettos: someone trying to make a positive life change, break the cycle, and take ownership of his or her life for the better is dragged back down into the vortex of violence, or into the life they're trying to leave, by someone who just can't stand to see them succeed.

But in real life, this syndrome is, sadly, more prevalent than the obvious examples of people trying to break free from gangs or ghettos. Lobster syndrome can be found in classrooms, offices, boardrooms, sports teams, neighbourhoods, yoga classes, and even churches, for that matter. And it is terrible.

"Watching someone else totally go for it can be incredibly upsetting to the person who's spent a lifetime building a solid case for why they themselves can't."

JEN SINCERO

Feeling that they themselves are not at a level of success they are happy with, or believing that they could/will never achieve their desired level of success, these lobsters attempt to pull down those who are aspiring for progress and are pursuing a higher level of achievement. They don't like seeing others becoming better than they are, and they negate any successful efforts of those very people, trying to make themselves come across as more favourable. This mentality stems from a place of insecurity, which develops into jealousy and resentment, and it is toxic to any environment in which higher-level performance or progress is the goal.

It is important to be able to identify lobsters and the soul-sucking toxic comments they make, however subtle they are or innocent they may seem. Although they are rooted in jealousy and blanketed with insecurities, those comments are an indirect kind of bullying, generating a fear of standing out and, therefore, potentially being *left* out—becoming an outcast. Identifying lobsters for what they are is the first step in disempowering them—both the comments and the lobsters themselves.

The girl I overheard in high school saying, "Look at her" was a lobster. Her comment caused me to avoid standing out, in fear of being '*called* out'. So I developed self-prescribed limitations in the interest of self-preservation. I let someone else indirectly dictate the direction of my future. Although I was the one in control, I had put a limit on my own potential with my choices.

If any of this sounds or feels familiar to you, know that high school is really just a microcosm for society—for similar issues we face throughout our personal and professional adult lives. When you hear people around you—especially those who are close to you—being spiteful and making fun of someone else, it is easy to think you don't ever want to be the recipient of that, and you bury your own ambitions in the sand. That you don't ever want to be that person in the corner being pointed out, so you just don't put yourself out there. These are the comments or behaviours that make us act in ways that don't align with our values, and that don't make us feel good. Because we are afraid of being judged, laughed at, or even yelled at. So recognize a lobster when you see one. And if it's not red with big front claws, sitting on your dinner plate—then avoid it!

Energy-Taker #2: Naysayers

Naysayers are not necessarily as malicious or as subtle as lobsters; they are simply disbelievers—people who do not believe in the possibilities of a particular outcome. They are skeptical and pessimistic, and liberally express their negative views, casting a sense of dismay, despair, and misery over a situation. They can be identified by their glass-half-empty attitude, which they try to instill in others. No matter how optimistic a situation may appear, a naysayer will point out the negative possibilities and everything that could go wrong, and emphasize the worst of a situation. In turn, people around them tend to question the possibility of achieving their desired outcome, 'catch' doubt (like one would catch a cold), lose hope, and often give up on their dreams. Having internalized the naysayers' comments, they rationalize their shift in perspective by having 'realized' that their goal was, in fact, a 'pipe dream'—they will change their goal to something more 'realistic'. Unfortunately, naysayers are everywhere and are equally as detrimental to you achieving your goals as lobsters.

CHOOSE ENERGY-GIVERS: THEY'RE CONTAGIOUS!

I have come to realize that by embracing the *discovery* of what you are capable of—pushing yourself and proactively pursuing a dream or a big goal—it subconsciously gives permission to those around you to do the same—taking away *their* fear of pursuing *their* goals because they know they won't be judged by you, as you are pursuing the same. This is in stark contrast to the effects of lobsters and naysayers. But positive thinking and actions can be just as contagious as negative ones. So limit the time you spend around energy-takers, and surround yourself with energy-givers—people who are excited about the possibilities of *your* life, not just their own, and who psychologically support you in your pursuit of personal growth, personal goals, and your best life.

"And as we let our own light shine, we unconsciously give other people permission to do the same."

MARIANNE WILLIAMSON

Rising Above the Energy-Takers

Shortly after I started training with the Canadian National Bobsleigh Team and pushing during pre-season sliding sessions, I overheard a coach tell my pilot/driver at the time that even though I was doing really well, she shouldn't focus too much on me and my development, or rely on me to compete in the Olympics. This coach thought that because I was new,

I could not be expected to do well under pressure against top international athletes, and so my driver should put her energy toward the other brakeman and use me as a spare. *That* is when I *confirmed* that I am fuelled and motivated by big challenges—the bigger the challenge, the better—especially those that would seem impossible to most people. Although I had succumbed in high school to a lobster, and had put limits on my own potential as a result, I learned later in life not to give in to the naysayers. In fact, when energy-takers try to bring me down now, it simply feels like a challenge.

What would you do if you overheard someone telling someone else not to count on you succeeding because you were new? Would you start believing them? Would you internalize what that person said and shrink away from the challenge? Would you start feeling and believing that your goal is not worth pursuing anymore? Would you start questioning your worth? I remember that around the time I heard those words I came across a quote: "Professionals built the *Titanic*. An amateur built the *Ark.*" Whether you are religious or not, that quote simply puts things into perspective: *never* discount what a rookie can do.

My teammate and I placed fourth in the Torino Olympic Games in 2006. Not bad for a 'rookie'. Less than five months after I jumped into a sled for the first time, we just missed standing on the Olympic podium!

Remember: Everyone you now look up to started as a rookie.

Camp ABLE: A Lesson in Rising Above

I lived and worked in Trinidad and Tobago for two-and-a-half years, from the fall of 2001 to the spring of 2004. Much of my work in Trinidad was as a Disability Sports Program Officer through Commonwealth Games Canada, which involved creating workshops, assessing schools, giving teachers and administrators advice on physical activities, exercises, and inclusion with respect to students with physical and developmental disabilities. I was free to implement what I wanted, and I wanted to embrace the challenges in front of me. I wanted to create something—something sustainable that would outlast my time there. I wanted to start a sports leadership development camp for children who were deaf or hearing impaired, and I wanted to call it Camp ABLE (Active Bodies, Leadership and Esteem).

There was no blueprint for what I imagined for this program, so I designed one. And my supervisor looked at my plans and, although somewhat paraphrased, said, "Well, good luck. You can work on it, if you want, but I'm not sure how you expect it to happen. I mean, where do you expect to get the funding for a project like this? I appreciate the ambitious nature of your thinking, but maybe you should focus on more realistic ideas that can be implemented."

Realistic! Ugh. This was going to be an even bigger challenge than I thought because I was dealing with a naysayer. Which of course only made me more determined.

I put together a small committee of teachers and others who knew sign language. Although I could have used the teachers to communicate my message, I wanted to *communicate* with the students myself. So I started taking lessons in sign language. It would have been easier to work only with local children, but when I thought back to camps I had attended as a child, I wanted these kids to have a similar experience—to have the opportunity to meet and befriend people from other cities and other countries. So I reached out to find schools in other Caribbean countries that would be interested in taking part. Even though I didn't have the money yet to book the flights or pay the deposit on the facility I wanted to use in Tobago, I talked to airlines about prices and seats, and convinced them to hold them for me until a certain date. When I had the numbers for all the parts of my plan, I established a budget and broke down the costs to what it would be to sponsor a child. And then I reached out to anyone I could who I thought would sponsor children for this camp. I went to companies, clubs, stores, and individuals, and presented my concept and plan. I talked to politicians. I asked all of them if they would donate and spread the word.

And then my first cheque arrived. It was from the Mayor of San Fernando, a city in the south of Trinidad. My supervisor looked at the cheque and the name on it and said, "I guess you can't turn back now."

Turn back?! I had never *thought* about turning back. I fought through his doubt, refusing to internalize it and make it my own. Instead of allowing it to create self-imposed limitations, I used his doubt to drive my follow-through and make this camp a reality. Trying to prove to my supervisor that it was possible forced me to search for solutions. And when it all came together, it was one of the most amazing things I have ever done, and one of the things I am *most* proud of accomplishing.

The first group of kids that first year came from Trinidad and Tobago, Barbados, and St. Lucia. I had arranged some camp-like outings and activities designed to increase leadership skills. I had also arranged for a local soccer team to play a game with the kids, working ahead of time with the players on how to communicate with the hearing impaired when it came time for the game.

When I flew with 'my' kids back to Trinidad, I watched as they ran to their parents who had been waiting at the airport. Their hands were flying, communicating excitedly about how they had played soccer with 'normal' kids and all the other things they had done at Camp ABLE. That was the most gratifying and rewarding moment of an overall remarkable experience: the excitement of those kids. And there have surely been more excited kids since then. Camp ABLE has been running annually by that local committee since that first camp in 2002.

It didn't matter that *no one* had ever done it before. It was like my first run in bobsledding (when I finally tried it)... just because I hadn't done it before didn't mean I couldn't do it or do it well. If I had listened to the doubts of my supervisor in Trinidad or the skepticism of my bobsled coach in Canada, and let their voices be louder in my head than my own, neither of those achievements would have happened. They were looking at the same situation as I was, but from a very different perspective, born from different past experiences. If you ignore the energy-takers and focus on the positive and the possibilities that exist, you will start to see solutions emerging through the disbelief and pessimism of others—it's amazing what you will see and can accomplish!

Highly Unlikely but Still *Possible*

When my teammate Kaillie Humphries and I arrived at the Olympic Games in Sochi, Russia, in 2014, expectations were high. We were defending Olympic champions, and only one Canadian athlete had ever successfully defended his or her gold medal before the Sochi Games in *any* Olympics. To repeat under that pressure was pretty amazing.

But winning in Sochi had a deeper meaning for me than you might think: even *getting* to compete in Sochi, let alone

winning a medal there, was extremely unlikely considering all the obstacles in my way and all the people who didn't
believe it was possible.

In the summer of 2012, after a winter and spring of track
cycling, both the rugby and bobsledding national teams
contacted me, asking me to return for their upcoming international events. It was a big decision for me, and it took me
the whole summer to come to a conclusion that I felt good
about. I decided I would return to competition. And I decided
I would do *both*.

I started to train again that fall, building up slowly, seeing
as I hadn't done any running for a year and a half because of
a serious ankle injury I got while playing in our last game at
the 2010 Rugby World Cup in England. Training was going
well and I felt like I was progressing, until about a month into
training when I developed pain in my right hip.

It was less than a year and half before the Games, so no
time to waste. I had an MRI and sent the images to Dr. Bill
Stanish, at the time one of the best orthopedic surgeons
in Canada. I knew him from some charity events we had
attended together. Surgeons are trained to look for things
they can fix, but I felt, because he knew me personally, he
would give me an honest opinion about whether or not I
needed surgery, or whether I could simply (or not so simply)
get by with ongoing therapy throughout the year. I believed he
would tell me if having surgery was *essential* for me to achieve
my goals of representing Canada on the international stage
again within the following year in not one but two sports.

He called me about a week later after receiving the images,
asking if I wanted the good news or the bad news first.

*Sweet! There's good news! Obviously if there's good news,
it means I don't need surgery. The bad news is probably just*

that I will have to deal with discomfort and ongoing therapy throughout the season ... So ...

"Hit me with the bad news first."

"The bad news is that you need surgery!"

Pregnant pause.

"Okay ... well, if I need surgery ... what's the *good* news?"

"Well, Heather, you definitely need surgery. The good news is that your hip is *so* damaged that you don't have to worry about having to make a decision as to whether you need it or not!"

Wow! Now *that's* perspective! Again, I needed to redefine 'realistic'.

I had hip surgery on November 21, 2012, performed in Halifax, Nova Scotia, by Dr. Ivan Wong (with whom I had gone to high school in my hometown). Since I was already an Olympic champion, I had plenty of acceptable options. I mean, most people would have seen hip surgery as a legitimate and understandable reason to 'gracefully' end my athletic career. I could have simply announced my retirement. I could have returned to a career in occupational therapy. Or I could have transferred my previous athletic successes into a personal training business or a career in television. I had people telling me I should quit while I was ahead because, well, what were the chances that I could actually win at the Olympics *again*?!

But for some reason, quitting just never occurred to me. To challenge myself and test what I was capable of, I disregarded the naysayers. And the odds. And focused on the possibilities instead of the unlikelihood of my desired outcome—on the 1 instead of the 662,000. As I've mentioned, I am motivated by challenges, which is why I had agreed to compete in *both* sports that year in the first place. And I knew I would need to do everything I could to get back in that Canadian rugby jersey and the CAN 1 bobsled again. I just never expected my challenge to start from a hospital bed.

The day after my surgery, a press release went out across Canada announcing my intentions of representing my country again on the international stage in rugby *and* bobsledding, defending my Olympic gold at the Sochi Games. I had seven interviews within a day. None of the reporters said I was crazy (at least, not to my face!), but they definitely questioned if I was being 'realistic'.

After all, making the Rugby World Cup Sevens team was highly unlikely. I hadn't played rugby in the two years since I wrecked my ankle, and I hadn't played sevens rugby (a very different version of the sport) in the almost five years since I had broken my shoulder in a tournament in Amsterdam. And the Rugby World Cup Sevens was only seven months after my surgery date. *Seven!* Highly unlikely!

Gold medal results at the Sochi Olympics? That, too, was *highly unlikely*! And it wasn't enough to just make the team. To have a real chance at gold, and be able to really *defend* our gold medal from Vancouver, I would have to be back in the CAN 1 bobsled again. That didn't look good either: I hadn't pushed a bobsled in two-and-a-half years; I was going to be thirty-five years old; there were only nine months from the date of my surgery until I would have to qualify for the national team heading into the Olympic season; and, on top of all that, when the press release went out across the country, Kaillie (my teammate from the Vancouver Games) had started a very successful season with another brakeman!

I was not entitled to that spot—I would have to earn it back. Kaillie and I won in Vancouver together, and we would always have that history. But that's all it was: history!

The only thing that was going to matter was *who* was going to get that sled going the fastest. But I had to be more than just fast. I was significantly older than the other women—by ten years in some cases. I had to make a significant *impact* and *prove* that I could add value. It wasn't going to be easy. But, then again, when had I ever gravitated toward *easy*?!

By this point, I knew what it meant to prove myself, to push past skeptics and naysayers, to earn my place, to lift the ceiling of what people believed to be possible. I knew I would need to rely on my ability of shifting perspective, and focus on all the ways it could go *right* while ignoring all the ways it could go wrong, to achieve what others said was impossible. It would take a lot of time, patience, effort, and discomfort. I would have to challenge my surgeon in terms of my rehabilitation protocol and to push my own limits—physically *and* mentally.

There were no guarantees that I would make the rugby team again. There were no guarantees that I would make the bobsled team again. Highly unlikely, actually. But . . .

And so I began the process: I rehabbed and trained my ass off.

I was on a stationary bike the day after my surgery. (I didn't have time to deal with scar tissue that could form due to inactivity.) I borrowed a muscle stimulation machine, which activated my leg muscles daily to prevent as much muscle atrophy as I could. Four weeks post-surgery I was doing pool workouts in a *very* attractive flotation suit—needed so I could do walking drills while avoiding active hip flexion (which, I was told, could cause the onset of tendonitis).

I worked hard at redeveloping and retraining all my stability muscles, and two months after surgery I was doing single-leg stability balancing drills while throwing a tennis ball against the wall and wearing strobe glasses. Yes, I said *strobe*. The glasses blacked out my vision at varying intervals (depending on the setting) just like a strobe light, with the intent to help my brain anticipate the trajectory of a rugby

Highly unlikely *does* **not** mean impossible!

ball, for example, that I might have to catch while being momentarily blinded by the sun. I also did the traditional therapies, such as physiotherapy and acupuncture. And I diligently followed the directives of my surgeon, living in my hip brace day and night for six weeks (although I *did* convince him to let me ditch my crutches after five days, saying they were more of a hindrance than anything). I did everything I could to get back on that rugby pitch and back in that bobsled.

But that's what you must do when pursuing goals that have no guarantees of success. You must aim to have the comfort and peace of knowing that you did everything you could to be the best that you could be at that moment—the moment you face the ultimate test of whatever goal you set for yourself. *I* knew that, regardless of my outcome, I could be at peace, knowing that there was nothing else I could have done. I faced the possibility that I might *not* make the team. Either team. But I did *not* focus on the possibility of defeat. I chose to focus on the possibility of success.

With all of that rehab and training, which came from my ability to keep things in a possibilities perspective, I *was* able to step back on that rugby field again, wearing a Canadian rugby jersey with pride. And seven months after my surgery, I was playing in the Rugby World Cup Sevens in Russia.

Nine months after my surgery, I had to qualify for the National Bobsleigh Team going into the Sochi Olympic season. At that testing camp in September 2013, I pushed faster than I'd ever pushed before! And not only that, I pushed faster than the other brakeman by two-tenths of a second—a pretty big margin in the sport of bobsleigh. And that meant that I was back in the CAN 1 sled again. And *that* meant I was starting my second Olympic season with Kaillie Humphries.

Just because something hasn't been done before doesn't mean it can't be done. It just means that the right person in the right place at the right time hasn't tried it yet.

AFTER OUR FIRST two runs at the 2014 Sochi Olympics, we were...losing.

We were the defending Olympic champions, and we were *losing*—by a lot!

Coming from behind to win a gold medal in our race? Highly unlikely! Whereas World Cup races are two heats on one day, results of bobsleigh events in the Olympics or World Championships are decided based on the accumulation of four heats over two days. And after our first day of competition (only the first two of four heats), we were 0.23 seconds behind the USA 1 team, which was at the top of the standings.

Now, 0.23 seconds may not sound like a lot to you, but it is an *eternity* in the sport of bobsleigh and Olympic time clocks! In my very first Olympic Games in Torino in 2006, after four heats down the track—a total distance of 5.7 kilometres (3.54 miles)—my teammate and I missed standing on the podium by 0.05 seconds.

Five one-hundredths of a second.

That is how close bobsleigh races can be: the difference between winning and losing comes down to a smaller amount of time than any human can even perceive! (After all, a blink of an eye is 0.3 seconds.) The only other bobsleigh gold medal won by Canada (1998) was actually a *tie* between the Canadian and the Italian men's two-man sleds. A *tie!* The margin of error is razor thin—about the time it takes for the single beat of a hummingbird's wing.

So, after the first day of competition in the Sochi Olympics, we were written off. We were no longer expected to win gold. I have it on good authority that even the CBC broadcasters commented among themselves that we had had a good season, and we should still be really proud of our... silver medals. *Silver!*

The race wasn't finished! In fact, it was only *half* done! I'm sure many others gave up on us too. I'm sure even more did when they read the *USA Today* article by Chris Chase, which made a comeback sound impossible: "Here's why the U.S. women's bobsled team has basically already won gold."

Sigh.

Now, I don't fault Chris for writing that. He was just doing what sports writers do. This was the story he wanted to write—the story he saw unfolding. He had given up on the possibilities of a comeback based on past experiences, which clearly helped to manifest his assumptions about what he thought could happen. He backed up the sensational headline by including a fact: "The leader after three [heats] has never lost a gold in the fourth." Well, up until that point, that may have been true. But as I've already discussed, just because it's never been done.... And then Chris quoted *Slate.com*: "Because bobsled results tend to be highly predictable, USA 1 might as well receive their gold medals now."

Poor Chris... ☺

He and everyone else who wrote us off didn't know we had no intention of letting him or anyone else determine the ending to our story. I hadn't completed my recovery from hip surgery in time to be there in the first place just to be written off halfway through the race. All the work I had put in. All the rehab I had done! All the missed weekends, birthday parties, weddings, and family events... Kaillie and I needed to push past the doubt and what experience was implying. *We just had to keep believing in the possibilities.* I mean, if USA 1 could make a 0.23 second difference in two runs, why couldn't we? Our perspective had to be unwavering: It might be unlikely, but it was still completely possible. We had to know that when it was all over we could look back and know that we hadn't given up before the race was over.

That we had given everything we had. That we had done everything we could.

That we had *fought* until the bitter end.

Despite what everyone else was saying.

AT THE BEGINNING of Day Two, Kaillie and I walked into the start house, found a place to drop our sliding bags on the benches, and started pulling out the things we needed to do our warm-up when I suddenly noticed Elana Myers—a truly lovely person and the driver of the USA 1 team in the lead—standing a couple of rows over. What I really noticed was some people going up to her, giving her hugs, and saying congratulations!

I spun my head around to face Kaillie: "Are you *seeing* this?"

"I know! She's already done an interview outside!"

"This is awesome!" I said. "They already think that they've won! And even if *they* don't, they still have to deal with the pressure of being in the lead. We just have to focus on us. Do what *we* do best. Let them make their own mistakes. We have *two* runs left. Two! We just need to close the gap a bit on the first one because then they might panic."

And after that third run, the gap *had* been reduced. By half. We were still behind, but we still had one run left. Gold was in sight. It was *possible.* But we had to stay focused on *us.* Back in the start house between the third and fourth runs, Kaillie asked me what the time splits were.

"You don't need to know the times. You just need to know that we've cut the gap in half. We just need to do the same thing again! It's possible! *It—is—possible!*"

And it was!

The *highly unlikely* story of coming from behind in the Olympic Games to win a gold medal in our race...

Achieving the *highly unlikely* goal of successfully defending our Olympic gold medals *in* that race...

And my *highly unlikely* recovery from hip surgery to even *be* there competing in the *first* place...

All *highly unlikely*—even written off—but obviously still completely possible.

2014 Sochi Olympics: Women's Two-Man Bobsleigh Results

CAN 1	57.39	57.73	57.57	57.92	3:50.61
USA 1	57.26	57.63	57.69	58.13	3:50.71 (+0.10)

TOO OFTEN WE let the naysayers dictate what is worth pursuing, based on *their* beliefs of what they deem possible. Had I allowed those who didn't believe that recovering from hip surgery in time to compete for Canada in the Rugby World Cup Sevens and the Sochi Olympics was possible affect *my* belief in the possibilities, I most likely would not have a Rugby World Cup Sevens silver medal or a second Olympic gold medal from Sochi.

In Trinidad, I held on to my belief in what was possible with Camp ABLE—my *goal* of an outcome I knew I would need to push myself to achieve but that was possible if I was willing to put in the effort and do the work. And back in Canada, I fought past the misguided belief that just because you're a rookie at something doesn't mean you can't succeed. Do you know how many times I've been a rookie?

DON'T LET OTHER people or circumstances cause you to 'dim your light' and downplay your talent if you are pursuing your passion. *Your* passion. And please notice that I wrote "cause *you* to 'dim your light'". Only *you* can allow other people or perceived obstacles block you—or not. *You* are in charge of your life and the direction it takes (or doesn't take). Remember? *You* are the driver! And *you* get to choose your destination!

5

OKAY... WHAT'S *REALLY* STOPPING YOU?

MOST OF OUR focus is on external obstacles, as it is much easier to blame our shortcomings on outside factors than on our own way of thinking. But *internal* obstacles are usually the real problem—the assumptions, fears, and self-limiting beliefs that make external obstacles seem insurmountable and certain outcomes seem unlikely. External factors are only obstacles if we *perceive* them to be—if we choose to see them as such. As I've mentioned, it's about perspective—about how you *choose* to react to the things that happen to you, to people, circumstances, events, and experiences.

Unfortunately, our internal obstacles are rooted in experience and are the underlying source of our perspective that dictates whether we see a circumstance or incident as an external obstacle or as a challenge. Your past experiences (even from when you were a child) are what create these internal beliefs to begin with, and they, in turn, determine how you perceive new experiences and whether you believe in the possibilities of achieving particular outcomes.

Experience

Injuries. Responsibilities. Environment. Finances. These examples are pretty obvious *external* obstacles—things blocking the likelihood of achieving a goal. But why on earth would I say that experience is at the root of the *internal* obstacles impeding you from your goals? Think about the experiences you've had—things you've witnessed, things you've learned, the consequences of your choices. Are they good ones? Do they empower you and give you a sense of confidence? Do they make you open to trying new experiences? Or are they experiences you'd sooner forget? Ones that you know have negatively affected your life? Ones you'd like to push permanently from your mind?

On the one hand, experience is a key element to learning, converting potential into skill and talent and turning talent into success. Experience enables efficiency, reinforces our accurate physical execution of skills, and teaches the consequences of certain actions—what happens if you choose to go down Road x versus Road y. Experience can also help you anticipate what might happen, and prepare you for obstacles that *could* appear. It tells you that, most likely, the sun will rise tomorrow.

On the other hand, experience can blind you from progress and prevent you from seeing and believing what is possible—from seeing choices and the potential within yourself and in others. What if the experience is a negative one? What if taking risks leads to disappointment and heartache? What if a bad experience contributes to a pessimistic outlook, and you believe as a result that you *won't* be capable of achieving a specific goal, that you will *never* become successful or that you will *not* have a safe, supportive place to land if you attempt and fail at something new? Experience may lead to learning, but at the same time, depending on what the experience is or how it is perceived, it could be a catalyst for internal obstacles (mental roadblocks) down the road.

BEWARE OF PAST SUCCESS

Just because all your past experiences seem to have been good and you've already experienced a certain level of success, it does not mean that you have achieved your highest level of success. I must warn you ... *because* you've been successful, you might just keep doing the same things over and over and never adapt, change, improve, look around you, and take things to the *next* level. You may be rooted in tradition, habits, or complacency that may actually be limiting or inhibiting your progress by preventing you from seeing other ways in which things *could* be done or improved. Imagine what could happen if you thought bigger, and believed in *those* possibilities—in what you are *truly* capable of.

The Ladder of Success

About a month before the Sochi Olympics, Kaillie and I were racing in a World Cup race in St. Moritz, Switzerland—the oldest and only naturally refrigerated bobsleigh track in the world. We had been having a great season and so were favoured to, at the very least, medal at this race. Steering is so precise, with such minute adjustments of the steering ropes (used to slightly shift the front steel runners), but a wrong steer, or doing the right steer too soon or too late, can have devastating results (crashing being one). Well, we didn't crash. But on the first run we *did* hit the roof in one big corner, which made us 'bleed' speed the rest of the way down the track. This one mistake put us four-tenths of a second behind the team sitting in first place. *We* were sitting in *tenth* place. Chances of medalling were impossible! Or... were they just *unlikely*?

I could tell Kaillie was frustrated about hitting the roof— totally understandable—but she was also beating herself up mentally (which would be the normal reaction of most athletes). She was quiet, keeping to herself, going over and over what went wrong in the first run. We loaded the sled onto the sled truck to be taken back up to the top of the track, and we climbed in behind it. I knew I didn't have to say anything about the run we had just done. And there was nothing I really *could* say about it. But I *could* try to shift her focus. So, instead, I took the pressure off and quietly spoke about our next and final run. "Just so you know, I don't care about winning... I couldn't care less right now if we win this race. But I sure as *hell* want to finish with a run that dominates this track. Let's lay down a wicked run! One wicked run! Who cares about winning?! Let's just finish with a run that people are going to remember!"

And we actually won! Without focusing on winning, we *actually* won! Never in the history of bobsledding has a team ever moved up so many positions. Fortunately, this gave us *experience* with coming from behind, so that when we were losing to the Americans by so much in the Sochi Olympic Games, we *knew* that a comeback and a win were... *possible*.

Your experiences can set you up for failure or success, making you *believe* whether you are capable or not... worthy or not... or whether you even choose to take the first step toward a goal. Your experiences can help you see an endless array of possibilities and opportunities that exist, or see only the limitations and deficiencies in your circumstances.

If I asked you what you would be if you could be or do anything, what would you say? Now wait! That sliver of a thought—that vision—that just crossed your mind? The thing you dismissed almost immediately after it entered your brain? What if I told you that *being* that is possible? That doing that *is* possible? Would you believe me? Or has your belief in what you are capable of been so deeply rooted in your past experiences and exposures that you simply can't see past them?

Assumptions, fears, and self-limiting beliefs are formed through the negative experiences you've had or witnessed others having—things that resulted in unfavourable consequences like failure, shame, judgment, disappointment, heartbreak (even if some of these consequences are only perceived, and not accurate interpretations of events). How many times have you thought you would never want to be in someone else's shoes because of something they had to go through or something you *imagined* they must be feeling based on a consequence—something you would probably try to avoid experiencing or feeling in the future.

Experiences, positive and negative, are precursors for the development of self-confidence and belief in one's abilities and potential to achieve one's goals—*or* the development of internal obstacles, blocking one's path to success.

The Upside of Experience

Experiences determine our belief (or lack of belief) in the possibilities and, therefore, whether we even choose to pursue a goal at all. Positive experience can motivate us to keep going, to forge ahead and succeed at what we set out to do. But not-so-good experience is the hardest thing to get past—the thing that gets us stuck in a limiting mindset and prevents us from believing in the possibilities of what *could* happen. If you truly believe that something is a waste of time, unachievable, or highly unlikely, then you will never get the most out of whatever it is you are doing. You will never reach your true potential because you turn your negative experience into a self-limiting belief, which becomes a self-fulfilling prophecy.

So, in fact, inexperience can sometimes help us avoid developing those limiting beliefs. Looking at a problem, challenge, issue, or new experience with fresh eyes—with a different perspective— can sometimes take your thinking or your actions to new heights by seeing possibilities that others may have overlooked.

Consider this example: Generally, people who built bobsleds either used to compete as bobsledders or worked as mechanics with teams for years—which is why bobsleds didn't change much for decades.

Then along came Michael Scully, a designer and creative director for BMW of North America who had previously raced cars and snowboards. In 2011, he took a ride down a bobsled track in Park City, Utah, and accepted the redesign challenge of shaving hundredths of a second off the finish times of the American sleds.

With twenty years of experience in building machines for speed, but absolutely no experience in building sleds, Scully entered into a six-year sponsorship agreement to build faster sleds. Instead of trying to make changes to the regulation bobsled in order to meet the rulebook's regulations, he went the other way: he looked at the rulebook and all its limitations and saw only possibilities.

Scully and his team built something very different from what was already out there. They did things that weren't in the rulebook because nobody had even *thought* about them. They changed the game and made things significantly faster because they weren't constrained by preconceived ideas of how things had to be. The possibilities Scully envisioned weren't limited by past experience. The only downside to this story is that my teammate and I had to compete against those American sleds in the Sochi Olympics, providing an even bigger *challenge* for us.

Just like Scully, my *inexperience* helped me in a number of situations: making the National Women's Rugby Team; creating a sports leadership development camp in Trinidad and Tobago; and making the 2006 Canadian Olympic Bobsleigh Team. Since I didn't know any better through past experience, I had no reason to believe those things were not possible.

Rookie vs. Veteran Beliefs

When I showed up for my very first bobsleigh race in Calgary on November 12, 2005, I didn't know we weren't supposed to win. I didn't know it was supposed to be hard. That may sound ridiculous, but it's true. I wasn't intimidated by the competition—I didn't know anything *about* the competition. To me, they were just other human beings—other women from around the world who were trying to do the same thing I was: push a sled the fastest and win a race. I thought, "Somebody's gotta win, so why can't it be *us*?!"

After all, I felt my driver and I were just as prepared as anyone. We'd been getting used to each other in training, I had learned the corners of the track and had studied the braking stretch, and I had learned how to take care of the sled and what to do with it at the bottom of the track after a run. I felt I knew what to expect and what I had to do to push well in the race. I was ready.

That first international race resulted in Helen Upperton (my driver at the time) and I tying the push-start record and finishing in third. Not bad, but I couldn't for the life of me understand why Helen was *so* excited. Or why the other drivers and brakemen seemed so surprised. Or why one of the coaches had tears in his eyes. There were hugs all around.

And all I could think was, "Umm... but we didn't *win*! Why is everyone so excited over third place?"

I didn't understand what it meant to be on the World Cup circuit, competing on the *world* stage, and to medal in a race for your country on your first try (or at all, for that matter). It wasn't just third place; it was third in the *world*. It wasn't until after the race that I found out that Helen—after four years of racing—had never finished in the top eight in a World Cup race before. I'm glad I didn't know that. Had I known, I might not have thought it was possible, therefore subconsciously lessening my effort. Or I might have put more pressure on myself (and may not have performed as well). But, instead, I was happily oblivious to it all. My inexperience worked to my mental advantage. I hadn't considered the fact that we were competing against Olympic and World *champions*. I hadn't even really thought about it as competing against the world—just as competing against other *women*!

Helen and I did four World Cup races together that season before the Olympics in Torino, and we medalled in every single one: that bronze in our first race, two silvers, and then a World Cup gold medal in the last race of the World Cup season. And then, only four months after jumping into a bobsled for the first time, I found myself competing at the 2006 Winter Olympic Games with every chance to build on that gold medal success. Standing on that podium was possible because . . . we would be *in* the race! There was no reason to believe we couldn't win.

And then we came in fourth. By that agonizing five one-hundredths of a second.

Helen was disappointed immediately after the race, but I felt fourth place at the Olympics after a five-month commitment of my life wasn't such a bad result. I tried to keep it all in perspective. But as the dust of the Olympics settled and weeks passed, I couldn't help wondering why . . . *why had we lost?*

It was the only race we had *not* medalled in that season, against the same competitors. Was it just that the competition was better that day? That everyone *else* suddenly stepped up their game? The numbers didn't seem to indicate that. So, what went wrong?

It nagged at me. Fourth place. So close and yet so far away. Five *one-hundredths* of a second.

Almost four years later, as the 2010 Vancouver Olympics approached, Helen finally told me why. Actually, she told the entire country why: *She just hadn't believed.*

The Canadian Olympic Committee had chosen the theme "Believe" for the Vancouver Olympics. TV commercials featured various athletes and their stories about how they believed in themselves and what they'd be able to accomplish at the Games. I remember sitting in my sister's basement in

Toronto when I saw for the first time the commercial that featured Helen. And I remember my heart sinking when she said that the reason we didn't reach that podium in Torino was *because she hadn't believed that she could.*

Why? Because it was the *Olympics*! Not because the other athletes were more talented, more prepared, or more equipped, but simply *because* it was the *Olympics*.

Helen's experience created a mental block for her. Her history of competing for years and *not* medalling, and the pressure she put on herself for simply competing on the Olympic stage, combined to undermine her belief that she could win at this most prestigious venue. This diminished the potential of what we were capable of achieving, by diminishing our collective belief in the possibilities.

In contrast, my perspective and belief in the possibilities had not been contaminated by that idea or by any past experience. Not having grown up really watching sports on television, I hadn't idolized Olympians or the Olympic experience so was not overwhelmed by the situation. Regardless, that five months of training and preparation went by so quickly that it was all a blur; I was so focused on learning this new sport and improving daily, on proving that I deserved to be there, that I didn't have the time or energy to worry about other people. I was so centred on what I needed to do that I don't think I even fully registered at the time that I was competing in the Olympic Games!

Besides, Olympics or not, we had beaten those same athletes, teams, and countries before on the World Cup circuit. My only past experiences with bobsledding were of Helen and I medalling in every race we had done together. The Olympics was just another race, wasn't it? *Somebody* had to win, so why couldn't it be us?!

It seems like Helen's perspective was that past results in the World Cup were irrelevant—the Olympics were different. To her, and to so many people, Olympic champions are untouchable—elevated to a place of admired unattainability (which is a notion, unfortunately, perpetuated by a number of successful athletes)—not everyday normal people like we considered ourselves to be. She had looked up to them as a child, and when she got to those Games, she couldn't grasp the fact that she was one of them—suddenly in that place of unattainability. Her long history in the sport, her idealized notion of the Olympics, and her past experience would not allow her to believe that she could stand on that podium too.

> "The only thing keeping you from getting what you want is the story you keep telling yourself about why you can't have it."
>
> **ANTHONY ROBBINS**

IT WAS ONLY in hindsight that Helen saw what could have been—although I feel that her immediately disappointment with our result was a reflection of her realization that we *could* very well have stood on the podium—but all it took to miss it was less time than a blink of an eye. Five *one-hundredths* of a second. Her limiting belief was based on her experiences and all she had been exposed to in the sport in the past, preventing her from seeing the possibilities as *actual* possibilities for her and for us. But Helen isn't unique. It happens to more people than you might think. Insanely talented basketball players who never make it to the NBA because they don't believe they're good enough to even go to a tryout. A brilliantly minded businessperson who never makes it to the corner office because she never took the initiative that she believed was reserved for *exceptional* people. Your limited belief in your own potential will always leave the door open for the TV people—those who *didn't* allow limiting beliefs to prevent them from pursuing what they wanted. How do you think they *got* to that top level? They always believed they were capable of way more in life, and they went for it.

You can't avoid having experiences in life and being exposed to different things and different kinds of people. The key is to shift your perspective to use that experience as a positive motivator rather than turning it into a negative, naysaying voice in your own head. What you achieve depends on how you view your potential in light of your life experiences. So don't look back in regret; believe in what's possible and work to make it happen!

IT'S ONLY HYPE!

At the 2006 Winter Olympics in Torino, Helen was caught up in the fact that it was *the Olympics* and she didn't believe winning was possible. This same limiting belief infected some of my teammates at the 2010 Rugby World Cup: they were so caught up in the fact that we were playing France (our nemesis) that they hyped themselves up and away from victory.

France was in Canada's pool as our last game before the finals started. And I knew we were capable of winning. France—the same team Canada had lost to in the last World Cup, the same team Canada apparently lost to every time we played them. And those results were very much in the minds of some of my teammates.

Although I knew we were *capable* of winning that game, as I looked around the locker room and listened to the various conversation, I could sense that we were going to lose. Let me explain. I knew the team had the skills needed to beat France, but once again, the burden of experience reared its ugly head, and they simply just didn't *believe.*

In fact, you might have thought the opposite of us that day as we took the field. My teammates didn't slump their shoulders or weren't talking about losing. But outward appearances and behaviours are not always accurate reflections of inner thoughts and beliefs.

My teammates pumped up the importance of the game so much that the overall vibration of the team was higher than normal. It seemed like everyone was panicky and frantic—like they were trying to convince themselves they could win. The players were so hyped up they couldn't bring themselves down. I heard people scream, "We've gotta treat this game like a final!" But *why?* Players looked at each other and screamed, "Now we need to step it up and PLAY!" But what did that mean? Hadn't we been playing to win in all our previous games?

My team failed to realize we were the same team on the same field we had been on before—that we were prepared, had a game plan, and would do our best to win because we want to win every game we play. And that anything is possible when you believe in the possibilities. My team was putting so much pressure on this particular game and moment that they failed to see that we weren't playing 'France'—as in the entire country—but just another group of women who had the same number of players as we did. Had the same goal as we did. Played on the same field everyone played on. Used the same balls we always used. Played by the same rules that we always played by. And they got no extra credit for past performance—it was a new day.

All my team could think about, however, was how 'France' had beaten us in the past. All I wanted to tell them was, "Don't let past experiences control what you believe to be possible in the future. Don't make a goal unattainable simply by elevating its importance either. Rely on your knowledge that you are *capable* of executing what it takes to win." But I didn't. Because I had been bobsledding, I hadn't been with the team—that particular group of girls—for as long as the team had been together. It almost felt like being a rookie again. Team dynamics is a big thing, and I felt like I was on the fringe. I didn't want to rock the boat moments before leaving the dressing room to step out onto the field. I thought, "Maybe this works for them. Maybe this has worked for them in the past. Maybe I should just focus on my own prep."

But we forgot who we were as a team and how far we had come by playing *our* game. We didn't play like ourselves at all.

Players made different decisions than they normally would have, getting penalties when they normally wouldn't have. We were playing like individuals instead of as a team. It didn't matter that we were 2–0 in the World Cup thus far and had won our first two matches 37–10 against Scotland and 40–10 against Sweden (far larger margins than France had won by when they were up against those same teams). The idea that 'France is our nemesis—we always lose to France' had already taken over the belief of what my team thought was possible (or impossible). And although the team sounded strong on the outside, it's hard to truly lie to oneself, and that collective thinking turned into a self-fulfilling prophecy.

We lost. 23–8.

Assumptions

Rooted in experience—and an offshoot of it—are assumptions. These are more sly and potentially damaging than the things that actually happen to us, the things that we actually experience, because we internalize our assumptions so deeply that we often believe them to be absolutely true.

An assumption is generally defined as a thing that is accepted as true or as certain to happen, without proof. We naturally develop assumptions based on past experiences, but the key here is *without proof*; assumptions are incredibly powerful in directing our thoughts and behaviour—and often in a negative, limiting way—but they are often not based in truth or fact. If it looks like a duck . . .

You may have heard the expression "When you assume, it only makes an *ass* out of *u* and *me*." To me, the most foolish thing is to limit your potential because of the assumptions you make about the situation, about yourself, or about what you are truly capable of. Without making decisions and goals based on fact, with 100 percent certainty about the outcome, there is always room for error—room to be wrong in what you believe to be true, room for your self-limiting beliefs to take over and decide what you can and will accomplish. People often don't even attempt a goal because of assumptions— based on the way things have always been done in the past, based on the perceived limitations of their situation (external obstacles) or abilities, or based on previous outcomes and consequences they have witnessed.

What is stopping you from tapping into your potential to see what is possible? Achieving what you want to achieve? Experiencing things you want to experience? What's stopping you from doing the things you want to do?

DURING MY VISIT home in the summer of 2016, my mother walked into the family room and proudly told me that she and Dad had added something to their bucket list. I was surprised to find out that my parents even *had* a bucket list. But I was, of course, also curious to know what they were so excited to have added, so I asked.

"To someday ring in the New Year with ballroom dancing in the Imperial Palace in Vienna," she told me.

Wow! What a great goal! "Are you going to do it this year?"

"No, we can't do it *this* year."

"Why not? What are you doing *this* year for New Year's?"

"Well . . . nothing. But it's probably sold out by now."

"Really? Are you *sure*? It's only July. Have you checked?"

"Well, no. But . . . it a big deal, so it would probably be . . ."

I picked up my laptop and within fifteen minutes discovered that tickets were, in fact, still available to attend the dinner and dance in the Imperial Palace ballroom. At the same time, Dad was checking out YouTube videos of the event, getting more and more excited with each passing minute.

With the newly discovered knowledge that it *was,* in fact, possible to attend the ball in Vienna, I looked up at Mom's surprised face and asked my parents if they wanted me to go ahead and book tickets for them right then and there. With the wheels clearly turning in my mom's brain, she leaned back in her chair and, after a brief pause, said it would be fun, but it would be *more* fun to go with another couple. I was single so it wasn't going to be me. So I suggested my Aunt Roberta and Uncle Alex, her sister and brother-in-law, with whom my parents had travelled to Germany the year before.

"They would be fun, but they can't go because they're taking a trip through the Northern Passage."

"*Really?* They are doing that trip over the Christmas holidays?!"

"Well, no. They are going earlier in the fall. But they wouldn't want to take two big trips so close together . . ."

I slowly smiled at my mother and asked, "Are you *sure?*"

She smiled back and said, "Well, why don't *you* call your aunt and explain the situation to her."

So I did.

After a quick phone call to my Aunt Roberta, I reported to my mother that she would run it by my Uncle Alex and would get back to her.

Not even ten minutes later the phone rang. It was Roberta announcing that . . . they were in!

We must learn to identify our assumptions for what they really are. And then challenge the *hell* out of them to discover which of them are *really* valid and which of them are merely stopping us from moving forward toward a desired outcome— for no good reason.

AS I MENTIONED earlier, when I was growing up I believed that Olympians were TV people, not everyday normal people like I considered myself to be. I subconsciously *assumed* that Olympians were *other* than I was and had grown up leading extraordinary lives. Many people assume the same thing about film and TV actors, idolizing them and forgetting (or not realizing) that most of them grew up in normal circum-stances. Many people assume the same thing about CEOs, high-powered attorneys, professors, and the like—that they must have had a special upbringing. Well, besides having grown up believing in their potential and the possibilities for their future, those people simply pursued a passion in their area of strength and *they* didn't assume good outcomes were reserved for *other* people.

Have you ever discovered that someone you knew growing up was doing something amazing with his or her life? And wondered how on earth they were able to do that, considering you used to be much better than them in that field when you were both younger? What stopped *you* from pursuing it? The assumption that *you* wouldn't be good enough? Why didn't you ask your crush out on a date? Because you *assumed* they would say no? Why didn't you try out for the varsity hockey team? Because you assumed you weren't good enough? Why didn't you submit an application for your dream job? Because you assumed you weren't qualified enough? What are you miss-ing out on by *assuming*? Perhaps a bucket list trip to Vienna?

But why do some people assume they *won't* get the date, *won't* get hired for their dream job, and yet still have no prob-lem pursuing those outcomes? The difference is *fear*. For some people, they fear the assumed outcome, or are so fearful of the *possibility* of a particular consequence that they avoid pursing what they want ... *just in case.*

Fears

Whereas assumptions can be based on the sometimes pure fiction that we create and tell ourselves when interpreting our experiences, our fears are usually very real because they are how we truly feel. And they are intimidating obstacles to overcome in pursuing personal potential.

I have crashed four times in my bobsleigh career. And, all things considered, they weren't very serious. But *one* of the crashes really rattled me.

It was during the 2007–08 season, on a track in Cortina, Italy, that was known for bad crashes. Even during our practice runs, I was thinking about crashing right up until the moment it happened because of its unnerving reputation.

We ended up rolling on a kink in the ice, but two quick corners later, before I could even think about options, we violently flipped back up onto our runners. My shoulder smashed against the side of the sled. My back went into spasm. And whether I was in shock or simply aware that we had just crashed on a track that was known for scary crashes, my mind was unsettled.

That night, I kept playing the scene over and over in my head, wondering what would happen if we were to crash again. I started imagining different scenarios, trying to decide what I would do. Would I bail out the back of the sled? Some people say that's the best thing to do on certain tracks. Others say *never* bail because you're still somewhat protected in the sled; if you bail and only get half out of the sled (with your shoe or speed suit catching on something), you could get dragged down the track like a ragdoll and crushed between the sled and the sidewall. All these possibilities ran through my head. I couldn't sleep.

When you crash, there are consequences of course. But how great? How much will a crash stop you from moving forward toward your goal? People on the bobsled development circuit often crash a couple times every week. When I tell them that I've had four crashes in my career, someone will inevitably tell me they had four crashes *yesterday*—especially if they are in driving school. (Yes, there is a driving school if you want to become a bobsleigh pilot. And, no, I have never had the desire to try driving.) They don't think crashing is crazy. They know it's part of learning. They know this "failure" is part of the game and is only as big a deal as you make it out to be in your mind.

If I let a fear of crashing control me, it would prevent me from giving 100 percent. And I knew if I weren't *all* in, consequences and all, I would not push my fastest. Even if I thought I was, there would be something holding me back ... even just a bit. Maybe just 0.05 seconds ...

I decided to race *despite* the consequences. Sure, I had gotten beaten up a little in the crash, and it could have been much worse. But the only way to step on that starting line and push as fast as I could the next time, with no inhibition, was to accept the possibility of crashing as a part of the sport, making a conscious choice that the risk was worth the reward. To me, the bigger risk was not going for my goal at all, not living up to my potential.

I made the intentional choice to go for it, knowing another bigger crash was a distinct possibility. This perspective— the awareness and acceptance of the possibilities, both positive and negative—is what allows you to give your full effort without hesitation. Three days later, Helen and I finished second—a World Cup silver medal—our best result so far that season.

I admit that after that crash in Cortina, I would still get nervous on certain tracks. Fear is a natural consequence of bad experiences and simply knowing more. But I decided never to let the nervousness own me. I would use it to fuel me instead. Pushing any less than my best would only be cheating myself and would in no way reduce the risk of crashing. If I couldn't accept and embrace all the possibilities that came with the sport—winning, losing, crashing, injury—then I shouldn't be doing the sport.

Fears prevent us from pursuing a goal based on the desire to avoid a certain outcome or consequence (which could be something we've experienced or just an *assumed* outcome or consequence). Fears come in all forms. Besides the fear of physical injury, most fears are social fears. People often don't take risks because they are afraid of failing. But this fear of failure is really rooted in the fear of being judged by others. The fear is of being shunned, isolated, disconnected. Without the possibility of being judged by others, failure itself wouldn't seem so bad, would it? You would just pursue what you wanted and, if you didn't achieve it at first, you'd simply try again. And again. And again. Setbacks only turn into failures if you let them get the best of you and you stop trying.

Yes, you may crash. You may 'fail'. You might even suffer an injury. Or you might just be disappointed in your result. But without taking a step and putting yourself out there, and putting your fears and assumptions to the test, you'll never fully tap into your potential and take steps toward fulfilling it. Reward inherently involves risk; to achieve your full potential, you have to push past the risk, the fear of failure, and take a chance on yourself.

"Too many of us are not living our dreams because we are living our fears."

LES BROWN

THE OBSTACLE OF INSECURITIES

As competitive as I was during all my athletic endeavours prior to bobsledding, I would only work on technical things and avoid extra training like weightlifting. But why? Why didn't I want to do whatever I could to get better?

Because I am naturally muscular and physically strong, I think people had always just assumed I worked out and lifted weights, which is probably one reason why I never did. I mean, if I already looked like I lifted weights, what would I look like if I really *did?*

Nowadays, weightlifting is one of the most common ways to change and sculpt the body to achieve a desired image. But when I was a teenager, having a muscular build for a girl was, unfortunately, not really considered to be the 'in' or 'attractive' thing—not really a highly sought-after look for women. Celebrity weight training programs were definitely not being profiled in magazines.

After some real soul-searching and self-realization, I've recently accepted that, not unlike many people, my insecurities were probably the biggest obstacle that could have prevented me from discovering what I was truly capable of and fulfilling my athletic potential. And not unlike many girls and women (and guys too, for that matter), I was self-conscious about my appearance.

I certainly didn't grow up that way. I mean, I never heard the word *diet* in our house unless it was referring to a balanced diet of all food groups. But in my later teens, people (including complete strangers) started commenting on the size of my calf muscles and asking me how long I had been lifting weights.

Although I don't believe any of the comments were *meant* to be negative, my muscular physique—a genetic hand-me-down from my father that included those huge calves—was commented on so frequently that I began to realize I was different, and it made me paranoid. If I started to lift weights, would I look like a guy—a huge bodybuilder? To add to that concern, I also had university football players telling me that they wished they had legs like mine. That may not seem like much, but combined with the fact that I was mistaken for a boy when I was seven years old, it certainly didn't help matters much. Stuff said to us as children has a way of sticking with us, doesn't it?

So I avoided the gym. Even at university, I would be given weight training program handouts from my various coaches and would simply toss them in the recycling bin when I got back to my dorm room. I mean, everybody *assumed* I was lifting anyway, so did it really matter?!

Again, it was about self-preservation—the desire to blend in and feel accepted. And knowing that my body was already different, I didn't want to do anything extra to make it stand out even more. The assumption that I would bulk up and look like a guy combined with the fear of being left out were the internal obstacles standing in the way of me discovering what I was capable of.

Some days I love my body. And other days I'm not happy with it at all. It's not always easy for a muscular girl to go clothes shopping. Sometimes I wish I had curvier hips or my shoulders weren't as broad. When I'm trying to buy jeans, especially now that skinny jeans are in style, I wish my calves were smaller (at least a little, so the pant legs would fit!). But my body is built for speed. And I am grateful for that, as it has allowed me to represent my country on three different international stages.

So whether you are wishing you were taller, had a thinner nose, had smaller feet, fewer stretch marks, more hair, a bigger bum or a 'six-pack' instead of a 'keg' (if you know what I mean), be grateful for what your body has allowed you to do so far in this life and for what it can do in the future—if you let it.

Self-Limiting Beliefs

"Don't be ridiculous—you could never do that! That's impossible!" You may think I'm referring to naysayers again, but I'm not. I'm referring to the little voice in your head that reminds you of all the external obstacles you are up against—your age, your weight, your previously failures, time restrictions, your lack of experience, your limited finances—and then somehow rationalizes these facts into legitimate *reasons* why a desired outcome can't be achieved. You may have been *rationalizing* for so long that you don't even realize you are doing it anymore.

Based on your past experiences, you might only see the way things have been done and who has typically done them, or how *you* have typically done things, instead of pushing past your predetermined beliefs and shifting your mindset to see new possibilities and choices that will help you achieve your goals.

When you ask young kids what they want to be when they grow up, they answer without reservations. Their answers are full of possibility: an astronaut, a police officer, a teacher, a pilot, a zoo-keeper... There is nothing in their past experiences indicating that these options were not possibilities. There is nothing that has given them reason to limit their beliefs of what's possible. Then, as we grow up, we are often told to focus on something more... realistic. But what does 'realistic' even mean?

The term *realistic*—which is generally defined as having or showing a sensible and practical idea of what can be achieved or expected—can be a limiting one, and I think we should be careful with how much we use it. Essentially, questioning whether a particular pursuit or goal is realistic puts a limit on the possibilities of the outcome occurring. But the term *realistic* is extremely subjective—based on a perspective developed through experience and exposure. Pretty soon we internalize the message that we should be more 'realistic' about what we can accomplish, and, before you know it, our interpretation of 'sensibility' and 'practicality' turns into a self-limiting belief of what is actually *possible*. And, sadly, we're telling ourselves to be 'realistic' all the time. But what if you shifted your perspective and your definition of 'realistic' was different—it *wasn't* a limiting one? What if it was dynamic and open-ended and continually evolved as you did? Maybe that shift would allow you to start dreaming big again, just like you did when you were a kid. Maybe that shift in perspective would enable you to see the *possibilities* that exist and empower you to challenge the boundaries of those previously defined limitations of what *was* considered 'realistic'.

What people see as being possible is a very broad spectrum. At one time, nobody thought it was possible to walk on the moon. Going ever *farther* back, nobody thought it was even possible to *fly*. What about the telephone—speaking

with someone on the other side of the world? *Seeing* someone on the other side of the world?! I bet the people who first
thought of those ideas were told to be 'realistic'. Because it
hadn't been done. And, now with the digital age, I think we're
realizing that there's no point in limiting the possibilities of
what we could see in the years to come in terms of technology.

The phrase *I can't* is more often a reflection of *I won't*.

IT IS NOT unusual in the sport of bobsleigh for teammates to
change between seasons (or even within a season), and at the
2010 Vancouver Olympics I stood on the top of the podium
accepting my Olympic gold medal with a different teammate, Kaillie Humphries. What about Helen Upperton? She
stood to my right, accepting her Olympic silver medal, with
her new brakeman, Shelley-Ann Brown. The experience of
coming so close to standing on the Olympic podium in Torino
four years earlier enabled Helen to believe—to *truly* believe—
that standing on that podium was a very real possibility. A
Canadian 1-2 sweep. In Vancouver. On home soil. Talk about
believing in the possibilities!

How much is belief worth? Five one-hundredths of a second? It may not sound like a lot, but depending on how your
experiences have been internalized, what you believe may
prevent you from realizing what you are truly capable of. Even
if that belief costs you less time than the blink of an eye, simply *believing* just might be enough to put you on the podium.

LIVING PROOF OF THE POSSIBILITIES

When you look at the adversities that some people have overcome in their lives, it shifts your perspective, allowing you to see the obstacles you face in your life through a different lens. Some of the most inspiring success stories are about people who have achieved great things despite the probabilities or odds of them not succeeding. Nelson Mandela was imprisoned for twenty-seven years and gained international acclaim for his activism, receiving more than two hundred and fifty honours—including the Nobel Peace Prize. Oprah Winfrey was born to a single mother, grew up in extreme poverty, and was sexually abused from a young age. She was fired from one of her early jobs as a television reporter because producers thought she was 'unfit for TV'. Yet, she rose to the top of that industry and was the first black woman billionaire in history. Michael Jordan was dropped from the basketball team in secondary school, and is now considered by many to be the greatest basketball player of all time. Malala Yousafzai was shot three times in the head for speaking out about education for girls and, having survived that ordeal, became an equal rights activist. She was named by TIME Magazine as one of "The 100 Most Influential People in the World" in 2013 and was a co-recipient of the Nobel Peace Prize. At the time, she was only seventeen.

Those are just a few examples of people overcoming adversity—overcoming the obstacles to achieving their goals—and they all have one thing in common: a fire inside of them that perseveres against any setbacks. They kept their goals as their priority, and have become an inspiration to people all over the world.

Pressure

Take a few quiet minutes to think about times you've stepped into competition—times you've put yourself out there to try to achieve a goal, whether it be starting your own business, going for a job interview, or negotiating for a promotion. Did you tell many people about it ahead of time? Or did you keep it to yourself in case it didn't work out? So you wouldn't have to feel like you let anyone down? So you wouldn't have to look like a 'failure'? Well, the pressure you feel when going after a goal in front of the entire world is a different story completely and yet not so different at all.

Pressure can come from thinking that people are relying on you to succeed. They could be parents, teammates, coaches, business partners, colleagues, friends, children, the *country*. This expectation is often perceived as an external obstacle, but it is, in fact, an internal one—the pressure we put on ourselves by adding a negative consequence to failing.

Think about it: Parents may want their teenager to do well in school, but if that teenager doesn't put any importance on school—not seeing a negative consequence to failing—nor does he care so much about pleasing his parents, he will not internalize the pressure and make it his own. He will not feel the pressure to achieve a certain grade.

Pressure usually has less to do with the actual expectations of others (external) and tends to come more from how you *interpret* the words and actions of others (internal). And it combines with a lot of the other obstacles I've been discussing to create a soup of feelings: the pressure you feel can be heightened by your *assumptions* of the consequences if you were to fall short of achieving your goal, which, as mentioned, is only damaging based on any *fears* you have about those assumed consequences. This is all relative, however, to how much you *believe* you will, or won't, be successful.

"Behind me is infinite power. Before me is endless possibility. Around me is boundless opportunity. Why should I fear?"

STELLA STUART

Therefore, pressure is *created* by any one or combination of assumptions, fears, and self-limiting beliefs. And it poses a threat to your success if you are unable to put those internal obstacles in perspective and manage them accordingly.

It is important to learn what the possible sources of pressure *could* be for you because they will inevitably impact your ability to perform at your best. To give yourself the best shot at success in anything you do, it's essential to identify and minimize the pressure you are carrying and its effect on your thinking. Of course, I recognize that some people perform *better* under pressure, and we all have our threshold. But, more often than not, it is stress and anxiety under pressure that leads to 'choking' under pressure, so learning to reduce the contributing stressors (or the effects of them)—by calming your nerves—is an overall benefit to performing at your best, whether it be competing at the Olympics or giving your best pitch in front of a potential high-value client.

Imagine you are about to give a presentation that could lead to a promotion within your company when suddenly you receive a text message from your spouse saying, "I know you can do it, babe. Bring home the money!" You're already feeling enough pressure, but then you start wondering how your spouse will feel if you, for some reason, *don't* get the promotion. Will he or she be disappointed? Angry? Now you feel

Success doesn't come from the absence of obstacles but from the appropriate handling and management of them.

way more pressure. Instantly your throat is dry and your palms are sweating, and you can't seem to remember your opening lines...

Earlier I mentioned that technology can be an external obstacle to achieving one's goals mainly because it may add unnecessary distractions that can halt or, at the very least, delay productivity and progress. However, technology can also enable an unnecessary feeling of pressure from people through social media—another type of external obstacle. And this kind of *distraction*—pressure—should be managed if you aim to perform at your best.

Although I sent out some social media posts from the Sochi Olympics to update friends and followers on what I was doing in the Olympic Village (this was only relevant for my Sochi Olympic experience, seeing as during the Vancouver Olympics I thought that Twitter was a useless fad that would soon be forgotten! I can admit when I'm wrong!), I consciously avoided reading tweets directed at me (or replies to my outgoing messages). Now, please understand that this is not usual for me—that I do, in fact, read social media posts that come through to me, responding when I can. Most of the messages directed at my team were supportive, excited, and expectant. But, that being said, depending on how a person internalizes any of those types of messages, they can help *or* hinder one's performance. Let me explain.

Social media opens you up to the comments and opinions of anyone and everyone—complete strangers who don't know you at all. That means that lobsters and naysayers have a direct platform to your 'listening' ear. Also, those who seem to be supportive may actually be adding pressure, making you start to think about 'What if?'...What if you *don't* succeed? What if I let those people down? Now, negative messages *may* be motivating for some if those people are driven by proving people wrong—if the messages fuel the passion—or they may have a negative effect on the psyche, creating doubt. Positive messages could simply be heart-warming and wonderful to read or hear, *or* they may add undue pressure to an already highly pressured situation.

If you don't think messages or the opinions of others affect you one way or the other, go ahead and read them. That goes for media headlines and articles too. But remember: *five one-hundredths of a second* can make the difference. And *that* can come from a split second of doubt, which could be subconsciously planted in your mind by a comment from a complete stranger—someone writing in *USA Today*, for example.

'BIG' EVENTS

Many athletes put more pressure on playoff games than regular-season games, hyping themselves up so much they can't focus on what needs to happen to actually win—too distracted to flawlessly execute the necessary steps required to achieve the desired result. Although training sometimes has to be adjusted leading up to big events—tapering to peak physically for the 'big' events—mentally, all competition should be treated equally. You shouldn't want to win any more in a playoff game than in a regular season game. Just like you shouldn't want to be a good parent only when people are watching. Or perform well in surgery only when a celebrity is on your operating table. If you don't perform at your best all the time, you won't know how to when those 'high-profile' moments present themselves. And then your anxiety will increase with the additional pressure you've put on yourself.

But athletes aren't the only ones who 'choke'. Getting too anxious, stressed, and hyped up is not a phenomenon that occurs in sports alone. It happens in life and in business when we put too much pressure on ourselves—faced with everything from a big test in school to a big pitch at work. We fail to see we have games and pitches all the time. That we obviously had the skills and the abilities to have gotten us to that point in the first place. Got a big meeting? Preparing for a big audition? Facing a big crisis? That word big is sometimes all it takes to lose perspective and fail to perform—execute—at 100 percent of what we are capable of.

It is those who prepare just as much for a 'small' meeting, pitch, or test as they do a 'big' one who are successful. It is those who treat all people alike, no matter their age, race, sexual orientation, socioeconomic status, or apparent social hierarchy, who are successful in leadership.

Chatroom 'Support'

Earlier I mentioned that in the spring of 2010, I had earned my way back onto the National Senior Women's Rugby Team to represent Canada again at the Rugby World Cup in England that August and September.

We had travelled to Wales a week before the start of the World Cup to train as a team, play a couple of friendly matches against the Welsh, and get over our jet lag. It was in Wales, on the team bus, where I realized just how damaging people's comments could be, as innocent as they may seem or be intended.

A young teammate leaned over the back of her seat to get my attention. She said she'd been reading all the comments online and told me not to worry because she "had my back" and was "standing up for me"!

What was she talking about? I had no idea. She explained that she had found a particular online chatroom where the conversation between these anonymous people was primarily about me, and whether I should have made the team or not—whether I *deserved* to be on the Canadian team at the World Cup. She said she wasn't the only one who was defending my position on the team, but that didn't seem to negate the fact that there were people who questioned it because I had been bobsledding and hadn't been with the team—that particular group of girls—for very long.

I didn't know how to respond. I think I told my teammate that she shouldn't be paying attention to chatrooms or any kind of chatter online or otherwise. She thought she was being supportive.

Although I *told* myself that that information didn't bother me, that it *didn't* have an effect on me, it had. I started doubting my presence there, wondering why the coaches selected me. Maybe the tries I scored *were* just lucky. Maybe I *wasn't* as good as I had been at the previous World Cup in 2006. Maybe I *was* only there to bring some media attention to the team because of my success at the Olympic Games only months earlier in Vancouver. Maybe I would disappoint everyone who was supporting me. Maybe I wouldn't even get on the *field*!

I was asked to do an interview a few days later for *Total Rugby*, a U.K.-based TV show. The camera crew showed up and filmed me taping my thumb (an old injury that persisted in needing attention) while chomping on my gum, going through some field drills with the team, and then sat me down under the rugby posts to do the interview.

It went well. Better than people would ever see online because I was able to take ownership of my thoughts again—give the proverbial middle finger to any doubts lingering in my brain. The ultimate rugby straight-arm (a tactic used by ball-carriers to fend off opposing players who are trying to tackle them by holding them away with a straight arm (locked elbow); also known as a *stiff-arm*).

When asked in the interview about my expectations for the tournament, I spoke about how skilled and ready our team was and how excited I was to be with the team. And then, although I didn't refer to the chatroom or the lobsters or naysayers specifically, I *did* mention that I was sure there were doubters out there, wondering whether I should be on the team. On international television, I admitted that those people were not thinking things that had not also crossed *my* mind, but that I had to trust the decision and insight of the coaches, and believe I was selected for a reason that would, in some way, help the team. If that meant stepping on the field again to try to score some points for my team and my country, then I would be honoured and would do it to the best of my abilities. But if my role was to bring water to the women who *would* be on the field, I would also be honoured and would do *that* to the best of my ability.

Announcing to the world that I, too, had had doubts worked to disempower them in my own mind. They no longer had control. *You* may not have a television platform to call out those who are affecting your mental game, but you can do that in your own mind. Internally acknowledge the pressures and expectations you are feeling, from others and yourself, ask yourself *why* you are feeling that pressure, and then put it all into perspective.

EXPERIENCING OBSTACLES THAT get in the way of achieving your potential is inevitable; learning to manage them successfully is essential to pursuing the path to your better self and your best life. Why? Because your beliefs, assumptions, and fears—all based on your past experiences—get in the way of you seeing the potential, the possibilities of the outcome that *could* occur. Instead of allowing external and internal obstacles to reinforce your own doubts—all the reasons why someone else would *obviously* get the job or promotion over you, all their strengths, skills, and advantages—think about *your own* strengths and resources, and all the reasons why *you* are deserving. Focus on the possibility of success instead of all the ways you could fail, which may discourage you from even trying to be your best. And then you'd have lost before you'd even begun.

If you believe things like lack of money, time, or support are preventing you from achieving a particular goal, recognize and accept that you are, in fact, using those things as excuses, sabotaging the possibility of achieving your goal. Your own thinking is the *real* obstacle—not the problem you are thinking about.

The key to unlocking your potential lies in your own mind, not in all the noise around you—other people, circumstances, experiences, or external roadblocks. It lies in your perspective and how you *perceive* the obstacles that will inevitably pop up along the way to achieving your goal, and in how much you believe in the possibility of achieving it.

PART

3

OWN

YOUR STORY

6

EXCUSES

Shift from Excuses
to Solutions

DO YOU EVER catch yourself making excuses when things don't turn out as you had expected or planned? Denying responsibility for events and circumstances in your life? Blaming them, instead, on things beyond your control? Have you ever tried to explain away why you didn't do something? Why, perhaps, you didn't achieve your goals? Not enough time. Not enough money. Not enough or the right resources. *I won't achieve them anyway. I don't know how. I'm too young. I'm too old. I don't like change...*

Well, excuses are not only rooted in assumptions (about what is possible, what resources are available, or the reaction of others) and limiting beliefs (about oneself or what resources are available) but are also profoundly rooted in fears—fear of uncertainty (including change) and fear of rejection (which projects as a fear of failure, fear of embarrassment, fear of success, fear of making mistakes).

And excuses prevent you from tapping into your full potential and discovering what you are truly capable of. They actually block your ability to recognize opportunities, see solutions, and develop the talents and skills you inherently have.

Worst of all, some people even start *believing* their own excuses, and start to justify them as being legitimate *reasons* for their actions or inactions. Those who specialize in excuses rarely accomplish anything.

Making an excuse is a choice. Not a great one if you want to be the best you can be, but it is a choice. To make the right choice for you, you must evaluate the potential consequences each and every time. How are these excuses stopping you from moving toward your goal? Why are you even *making* excuses? What are they protecting you from? Or do you really *want* it that badly? If it *is* a goal you truly want, why haven't you achieved it yet? As Arnold Schwarzenegger has said, "You can have results or excuses. Not both!" The good news? It's your choice!

If you don't want to go to the gym, just say so. But don't say you don't have time. We all have the same amount of time. Technically, you are just prioritizing something else above going to the gym. And, if that's the case, that's totally fine. Just *own* it! But also know that every choice has a consequence, so be sure to keep your ultimate goals in mind when making your choices.

So, the first step to 'owning your story' and achieving more than you even thought possible is to take the blinders off. Stop seeing only obstacles where opportunities also exist. And stop making excuses based on those perceived obstacles to your success. Shift your perspective, look for the positives in every situation, and move from excuses to solutions. Making the intentional choice to make a change for the positive in your own life is key to tapping into your potential.

"You can have results or excuses. Not both!"

ARNOLD SCHWARZENEGGER

BEFORE I MADE the National Women's Under-23 Rugby Team in June 2000 at the age of twenty-one, I didn't even know there *was* a National Women's Rugby Team until I was told, after a tournament the summer before, that I had been added to the national long list. Suddenly, I had to find a way to prepare for a couple of games we would be playing against the United States at the end of that summer. But I was living and working in Halifax for the summer, and the women's rugby teams there, at the time, didn't start training until just before the fall season.

So I found a local men's rugby team and asked if I could train with them. I didn't want to get in their way, but I couldn't very well pass the ball to myself, could I?! So I explained my situation to the captain, and ended up joining the Halifax Tar Heels for the summer. I had about twenty big brothers looking out for me, who were as excited as I was about my opportunity to represent Canada later that year. It was extremely physical, and training with those guys *really* pushed me. It was the best thing I could have done. No excuses. Just solutions.

In the summer of 2009, I was home visiting my parents in P.E.I. during my training for the upcoming Winter Olympics in Vancouver. I had an upper-body workout on my training schedule that, to be perfectly frank, I didn't want to do. I went to the gym anyway. But when I showed up, it was closed. I tried the door and it was locked. I then saw the notice on the door: *Closed for the holiday.* Now, had I been in a bigger city, the gym would probably have been open, but I was in Summerside. I was actually relieved. *So* happy. Probably more so than I should admit. But I had been craving a day off like people crave chocolate, and I thought it was a sign: maybe I deserved a break. The locked gym door was the perfect excuse. So I went home with a big smile on my face, kicked my shoes off in the back hallway, flopped onto the couch in the family room, and picked up the TV remote control.

And then, just as my body started to melt into the cushions, out of nowhere I suddenly got a vision in my head of the other woman who was fighting for my spot on the Canadian team. I just *knew* that she was at the gym somewhere. I mean, she lived in Toronto. *The gym's not going to be closed there . . .*

> 66If it is important to you, you will find a way. If not, you'll find an excuse.99

RYAN BLAIR

Your excuses reveal your priorities.

I started thinking that if I didn't do this workout and didn't make the team, I would regret it. I would look back on this moment and it was going to haunt me. I put my shoes back on and started to go out when Mom stopped me and asked where I was going. I told her I was going up to the school. Mom looked confused, knowing that the school, too, would be closed for the holiday. But I was determined to find *something*.

I walked a block up the road to an elementary school and did an entire upper-body workout on the playground equipment outside. Not the same workout I would have done in a gym, but I did *something*. And I left that playground feeling fatigued and satisfied, knowing that I was doing everything I could in pursuit of my goal. There was nothing more I could have done.

But I also left that playground realizing how excuses really *are* everywhere.

And that we really are all capable of *way more* than we give ourselves credit for. We so often sell ourselves short and allow excuses to become justifiable *reasons* in our minds for why we didn't reach our goals. We are faced with an obstacle—a locked gym, for example—and see a *reason* instead of a challenge. Instead of making an excuse—justifying the obstacle standing in your way—make the choice to do something that moves you forward, pushes you, gets you one step closer to your goal. Excuses are choices. They are choices that we so often regret in hindsight. Choices that move us further from our goals.

I could easily have *rationalized* missing a training session with the fact that the gym was closed, and that would have been an acceptable *reason* for almost anyone. But . . . *I* would have known. *I* would have stood at that starting line at the Olympics *knowing* that I had not done everything I could to prepare. *Knowing* that my opponents probably did more. And *that* would have affected my confidence—my *belief* in the possibilities. And *that* could have cost me... five one-hundredths of a second!

I wanted to stand at the top of the bobsleigh track in Vancouver and know that I had done everything I could to be the best that I could be at that moment. To be able to know at the core of my being that I had done everything I could in pursuit of my goal. That way, regardless of outcome, I could be at peace, knowing that there was nothing more I could have done. I would be able to look back on my journey and have no regrets.

Having no regrets means having no excuses! It means being able to look back at every choice you made, every action you took, every word you spoke, and know that you did everything you could to be the best you could be when it mattered most. By living up to your full potential, or at least trying your best to, you will be far less likely to have regrets than if you settle for mediocrity, the easy path, or don't push past the obstacles and excuses that stand in the way of achieving your big goals. Every choice I made en route to the Olympics was with my final goal in mind. No excuses. No regrets. Peace of mind.

You will achieve your goals when they become more important than your excuses are powerful.

7

CHOICES

Shape Your Life One
Choice at a Time

EVERY DAY WE are faced with thousands of choices—the building blocks of our life stories. They determine which path we will take when faced with a fork in the road. Choices govern where our life will end up, and how we get there.

I am proof that each choice, however big or small, can change the course of your life. I always considered myself to be a 'normal' person, from a small town in a small province, and yet I am now a two-time Olympic gold medallist and World Rugby Hall-of-Famer, joining fellow hall-of-famers Johnny Wilkinson and Nelson Mandela! Looking back, I find it all very surreal and strange, and I realize that none of it happened overnight or by accident; it all happened because of countless individual choices I made about my life along the way. What choices have you made to be where you are now? What choices can you make now to move you closer to where you want to be? How will you choose to shape your story?

But *owning* your story sounds easier said than done, doesn't it? I mean, we are constantly bombarded with choices, and some of them involve life-altering options. How many choices—and decisions—do you think you have already made today? Regardless of whether it is choosing the colour of our socks, which program to attend at university, or whether to accept a blind date (these days as simple as 'swipe left or right'), our decisions ultimately shape who we are.

Okay, not every choice is worth struggling over (like the colour of your socks); but making larger choices without being self-aware or mindful may result in you floating through life, settling for mediocrity rather than making conscious decisions and choices to make your life the best it can be—for you.

MY DECISION TO pursue bobsledding was not exactly what one would call a mainstream career choice. But when I *did* choose to pursue it, I chose a path of unpredictability— unpredictability in outcome, unpredictability of income (or predictably limited income). I was passing up the opportunity to work as an occupational therapist, and the security of knowing what I would be earning every year, the stability

Repeat to yourself:

"My life is the result of the choices I've made. My future will be the result of the choices I make from this point on."

of living in one place, and the low-risk career of working in a hospital or community position—not hurtling down an icy track at speeds of up to 150 kilometres an hour.

At first, it was simply the challenge that motivated me—seeing if I could learn a new sport, learn to do it well, and learn to do in less than five months, in time to represent Canada at the next Olympics in Torino 2006. In my mind, it wasn't a matter of choosing bobsledding over a career in occupational therapy, but, rather, a choice to put my master's degree and OT career on hold for a year. A one-year leave of absence was all my bobsledding adventure was ever meant to be.

But when my teammate Helen and I missed standing on the Olympic podium by only five one-hundredths of a second, *that* led to another fork in the road—another choice that had to be made: go back to school and finish my OT degree as planned or push forward to the 2010 Vancouver Olympics and try to make that podium.

To me, it was a *non-choice*... at first. Although I *did*, ultimately, have a choice, I did not seriously consider the option of continuing bobsledding because I had already made a commitment to myself before my leave of absence to return to school to finish my master's. Education was (*is*) important to me, and that path was, I thought at the time, *real* life—the path to how I would make my living.

So I kept my commitment. I went back to finish my degree. But by the end of the program that following year, questions nagged at me: Did I really want fourth place to be my story? Forever?! We had been *so* close to standing on the podium—the epitome of the saying "so close and yet so far away".

Placing fourth felt like unfinished business. And, with the next Games on home soil, it was enticing. I mean, we were able to place fourth after only five months of training; what could we do with three years?

In the end, I decided I didn't *want* fourth place to be my story.

Especially if I *knew* I was capable of so much more. I didn't want to look back and wonder what *could* have been.

So I made another choice: to go back to bobsledding. To see what was possible. Was success a guarantee? No. The future of any true story in real time is always unwritten. But our choices define the path we take. The decisions that we make—both big and small—shape who we are and the direction and story of our lives. Every single decision you make along the way has to be made with your goal—those final pages of your story—in mind.

Your choices define you. Who you are today is a result of the choices you made in the past, and your future will be a result of the choices you make today. That may sound oversimplistic, but that's exactly how life works. What you choose to do each day will determine the kind of person you will become and the extent of your success and self-fulfillment.

So how will you push through the excuses and doubt to take control of the path your life takes? How will you write your own story? What choices will you make to shape the story and the life you want?

Be conscious of your choices. Be mindful of the implications and intentional about your decisions. Because every choice has consequences.

Your life. Your story. Your choices.

8

CONSEQUENCES

Take Responsibility for
Your Choices

THE STORY OF your life starts with a choice and is shaped by the consequences of your choices. And the story that will be told at your funeral will be the result of choices. *Your* choices.

When I was young, I used to read *Choose Your Own Adventure* books. You know, the ones in which the narrative brings you to a dramatic situation—a fork in the road, sometimes literally and sometimes figuratively. And you get to choose. Depending on which option you choose, you are instructed to turn to a specific page to continue the story... until you come to another decision-making point, at which time you have to make another choice. And so on. How the story ends is based on the choices you make throughout the book.

I didn't realize it at the time, but I was getting a lesson on choices and consequences. Unfortunately, however, it seems that people aren't reading those books anymore... because they don't seem to be taking an active-enough role in charting their own life's journey. Maybe it's just me, but people nowadays seem more content to let life happen *to* them and are less motivated to take responsibility for what happens in their life. Call it entitlement, call it complacency. Whatever you call it, people need to own the consequences of their choices. *You* are responsible for how your life will unfold. So if you haven't already, start now and own your choices, own your consequences. *Own your story!*

Those *Choose Your Own Adventure* books were not the only place where I was learning about the consequences of my choices. My siblings and I grew up learning important lessons about taking responsibility for our actions.

Not making a choice is actually a choice. And every choice has consequences.

ONE DAY, WHEN I was six years old and my brother was three, our friends from across the street came over to play. We were hanging out in the family room when my brother disappeared and came back a few minutes later with a bunch of Arrowroot cookies (technically referred to on the box as 'biscuits'). He handed us each one. I ate mine quickly, and then immediately went into the kitchen to find my mother, the obvious source of the cookies.

"Mom, Walter didn't give me a cookie."

"He didn't?"

"No."

"I gave him one to give to you."

"Well, he didn't give me one."

"Well, what do you think he did with it?"

"I don't know. Maybe *he* ate it."

"So you're telling me you did *not* have a cookie?"

"Right. So can I have one?"

"Come with me."

My mother took my hand and led me down the hall and into the bathroom. She boosted me up so I could see myself in the mirror. I had crumbs all over my face.

I had to tell my friend that she had to leave because I had told a lie.

Lying is a choice. I had hoped for the consequence of another cookie but ended up with the consequence of a punishment. Consequences provide us with experience from which we can determine actions with more favourable outcomes in the future. We can learn a lot from consequences. Unfortunately, the consequences of that little lie were note enough of a deterrent to prevent me from lying again . . .

WE WERE IN Halifax, Nova Scotia, and Mom said that we could go to the Public Gardens to feed the ducks. I was so excited. She told me to go to the bathroom before we left. I went first, and then Mom went and came back out. As most moms do, she asked me if I had washed my hands. *Yes*. And if I had used soap. I told her I had. But, apparently, there had been no soap at all in the bathroom.

I was busted. And going to the Public Gardens to feed the ducks was no longer on the agenda. *That* was the last time I lied to my mother.

If you call out your own excuses... If you make intentional choices... Just think about what you could achieve!

A CONSEQUENCE IS the feedback we need to learn in order to modify our behaviours and improve. When I skipped in the house to show my grandmother what a good skipper I was, I knew we weren't allowed to skip in the house even if she did not. And when I knocked something over? I wasn't allowed to go to a friend's birthday party that afternoon. Not because I knocked something over, but because I broke the rules. My grandmother was blown away by the fact that I didn't freak out about having to miss the party. It was my fault and I knew it. In my family, we knew the rules and the consequences of breaking the rules. We were 100 percent responsible for our actions. I never skipped in the house again.

In hindsight, I am grateful for the uncompromising consequences I received from my parents for my actions. I learned about accountability and how to take responsibility for my choices. When I was late for curfew during my high school days (which, I must say, only happened a couple of times), Mom and Dad actually sat me down in the living room and asked *me* to choose an appropriate consequence! My parents have since told me that we, as kids, always chose a bigger punishment than they would have chosen for us! Ha! I guess by that point my siblings and I already understood that choices have consequences, and knew that we would have to take responsibility for our actions. We all learned at a young age that we were accountable for our actions and our choices, that each of us is responsible for our own life.

That is *not* to say that I have never made mistakes or what would be considered a 'bad choice', or that I never neglected to think through the consequences of my actions...

DURING MY SECOND year at university, I had to take Statistics. It was a mandatory class for my program. Not only did I not enjoy the class, but it was at 8:30 a.m. three times a week. We also had a textbook from which the prof was taking his material almost word for word. So I thought I could just do it on my own. A couple of weeks into the course, I proceeded to snooze my alarm clock (multiple times) and missed weeks in a row of the class. When I finally *did* return to that class, I realized that I had *no* idea what was going on and couldn't understand a thing. The class was too far along. I failed the course.

It didn't matter that the prof was the faculty advisor and had given me misleading information the year before that had led to an unnecessarily stressful year. Although I wanted to blame him, it wasn't his fault that I failed. Hitting that snooze button was a choice. It was *my* choice. A choice I, unfortunately, made too many times. I just didn't consider the extent of the consequences. I thought I was simply compromising a really good grade for an acceptable one—not compromising the whole class.

Trust me, you never want to have to take Statistics twice.

I LEFT HOME at the age of eighteen to start the first year of my undergraduate degree at the University of Waterloo. That, in and of itself, was a difficult choice, but I based my decision on a few things: I wanted to leave the Maritimes (even temporarily) in order to experience life *really* away from home; the

program I wanted—a science-based kinesiology program—
was pretty reputable at that university; the University of
Waterloo was a highly ranked academic university; and they
had a nationally recognized track program with an amazing
coach, and I thought it would be cool to see what I could do
with just some technical training for sprinting.

One element in making good choices is due diligence: getting all the information you need to make the right decision
for you. As I mentioned, I certainly don't regret the decision
to go to the University of Waterloo, but I discovered when I
got to campus at the start of the school year (never having
visited before as it was a few provinces away) that the school
didn't even have a track! The track team trained in a hallway
behind the bleachers in the gym, doing wind sprints full tilt
into crash mats that were leaning up again the wall at the
opposite end of the hall. Who knew?! However, you make the
best choice you can with the information you have at the time,
and you live with (and make the best of) the consequences.

WHY DO YOU choose to do the things you do? I mean it. Why?
Why do you *really* do the things you do? And yes, there is a reason. And yes, it *is* a choice. It is *always* a choice. And choices
always have consequences. They go hand in hand. So, when it
comes down to it, it is the consequences of our choices—the
consequences of our actions—that help us make our decisions
going forward. And the countless decisions we make, knowingly or unknowingly, are vitally important to our level of
success *and* our level of happiness and sense of fulfillment.

Why do you choose to do the things you do?

9

NO REGRETS

Make Decisions that
Are Right for You

HAVE YOU EVER bought an article of clothing that's tagged "one size fits all" only to try it on and realize, "Yes, it does fit my body, but it certainly does not look good!"? It fit, but it wasn't the *best* fit. Well, in a way, that's the same as choosing the path to pursuing your goals. There is more than one way to achieve a goal, but you have to find the path that is the right *fit* for *you*. What works for some people (and possibly *everyone* else) may not work for you at all.

Sometimes you have to dance to the beat of your own drum. Sometimes you will have to make decisions that don't align with what other people see as being the only way of doing something. Remember: Some people can only see three sections of the beach ball, and won't be able to see other solutions unless you help shift their perspective. But the only way a decision will be right and feel authentic for you is if it aligns with your priorities and, most importantly, your values.

Values are at the heart of authenticity. And they are central to figuring out what path to your best self is right for you. What does it mean to be authentic? An *authentic* piece of art is so-called because it is an original—not a copy or a fake. It means being genuine—being able to express your inner self openly and honestly.

Many people present themselves to the world in a way they think others would approve of, in a way they believe is most acceptable, or sometimes in a way they believe would be most advantageous to them. Many people just go with the flow, not wanting to make waves even though they know it's not right or know there's a better option. They pretend to be okay with the situation. Whether they are aware of it or not, they are pretending to be something they're not. They're not being true to themselves, so they are not being authentic.

But why? Because of fear: the fear of being judged and criticized, or not liked, wanted, or accepted. Do you remember a time when you expressed your true thoughts or feelings, which were quickly dismissed, made fun of, or cut down? Of course, you do. Everyone at some point has experienced this! But if you want to reach your potential, you have to move past that fear and embrace your authentic self because the path to fulfillment begins with authenticity. Being authentic starts with truly knowing yourself. It means getting in touch with your *real* feelings, needs, desires, and values, which may very well have been buried for a long time.

"Our lives improve only when we take chances— and the first and most difficult risk we can take is to be honest with ourselves."

WALTER ANDERSON

Authenticity: Being True to Your Values and Priorities

Your values are central to who you are and who you want to be. Whether you recognize it or not, you have a hierarchy of values that consists of things such as health, security, wealth, family, meaningful work, status, happiness, creativity, service, and countless others. Values are the things that you believe are important in the way you live your life, and they determine your priorities. This hierarchy is the foundation of how you make your choices. Salad or fries? Stairs or escalator? TV or time spent on personal development? Evenings with family or working on an extra project to get a promotion? Gym or an extra hour of sleep? Use end-of-year bonus money to buy a nicer car or invest it?

As your definition of success changes, so will your personal values. And, in turn, so will your priorities. For example, working a seventy-hour week might have been fine at the start of your career when one of your primary goals was acquiring money and status; but it may no longer be a priority once you start a family of your own, when you are putting work-life balance higher on your hierarchy of values.

Although some values can conflict with each other, when you identify your own personal values, you discover what's really important to *you*—not your boss or your in-laws (which may, at times, feel like one and the same). It is important to identify your own values because this knowledge brings clarity, and helps you to make choices about how you live your life—the best, most authentic choice for *you* in any situation. Should you accept the promotion? Should you quit your current job to start your own business? Should you follow your heart?

I no longer minimize my efforts when pursuing a goal. I know what is important to me, and I have learned to identify excuses and evaluate options and consequences to make authentic choices that I won't regret in hindsight. I own my story. My life is the result of the choices I have made, and my future will be the result of the choices I make from this point on. The possibilities for my future lie in the steps I decide to take toward fulfilling my potential. What choices are *you* going to make? Will they be true to your values? Even if they're not always easy to make?

People may ask you what accomplishments you are most proud of. But I want you to think about what *choices* you are most proud of. Usually those are the choices that take a lot more thought, they are much more intentional, and often go against the expectations of others. But they are usually made because they align with your true values, your true beliefs, and are usually the ones that are the hardest to make. They feel the best because they are authentic.

Sometimes we *feel* like we have to choose between feeling like a failure and feeling like a fake. Choosing to be authentic can be risky because you may be taking the road less travelled, or the goal you're shooting for may be so lofty that you discover that you simply *can't* attain it. But not going for it, not being true to your authentic self and pursuing your passion, can result in a lack of meaning and fulfillment in your life.

Now, I didn't say living authentically and making values-based choices would be easy! But knowing your values, and making a choice that you know is right for you, is a lot less difficult to deal with in the long run.

"You have brains in your head and feet in your shoes. You can steer yourself in any direction you choose!"

DR. SEUSS

THERE IS A downside to going with the flow, making choices based on the dreams and expectations of others and the pressures of society instead of making conscious, intentional choices that are connected to your own values, goals, and definition of success. Don't choose an option simply because you believe it will get you further ahead. Because it might do just that. I mean, it might very well move you further ahead but on a path that's not authentic for you and, therefore, not headed toward the destination you truly want—the life that will make you the most fulfilled.

I know a very successful defence attorney who lives and practices in Toronto who is miserable in her job despite outward appearances. Unfortunately, this is not an isolated case and is more common than people would like to admit. Someone asked this lawyer if she would sit down with his son to give advice on pursuing a career in law. She didn't see how she could refuse this favour that was being asked of her, but she was anxious about what to tell the young, optimistic university student. To the rest of the world, for all intents and purposes, she was very successful; but she was unhappy—she hated her job and was living a life she never really wanted.

How did she get to that point? I never asked. But one can assume that incentives that seemed appealing at the time simply didn't align with her true values and priorities, and the momentum of accomplishment led her to a place where she didn't recognize herself anymore.

In other words, being successful and *feeling* successful (fulfilled) are often, sadly, two different things.

There are pressures everywhere. People are so concerned about 'missing the boat', about being different, or taking a risk to get what they truly want that they cannot bring themselves to veer away from the crowd and make their own choices. Parents, too, feel the pressure to conform, inundating their children (and themselves) with games, practices, lessons, and other activities on top of their own work (and hobbies, if there's any time left); but they are afraid of taking a different path, and saying no to things in the off-chance that it will somehow negatively affect their children in the long run.

But what about looking at things the other way? I mean, stress and anxiety disorders are now being diagnosed in young children. Maybe less is more? Maybe *not* staying late to work in the evening is the right answer for you—doing your job to the best of your abilities, but prioritizing your time at home in the evenings with your children. There is not one right answer that fits for everyone. But clearly defining what success means to you, identifying your values, and your priorities, and being aware of the obstacles to achieving that success will help make your choices a lot easier. You won't be influenced by what is important to *other* people—you will stay focused on what is authentic and important to *you*.

Family Day: Values in Action

Some of life's choices really help shine a light on what you value most. When you are confronted with many options that seem reasonable, clarity about your values and priorities is helpful and comforting, and can be used as a strong guiding force to point you in the right direction.

Growing up, I never practised with any sports teams on a Sunday. This was not because my coaches never held a practice on a Sunday but because my parents told my coaches at the start of every season that if they held a practice on a Sunday, I would not be there. This was not because they didn't care about sports or because my being successful in sports was not important to them. Their decision had nothing to do with sports per se. It was the same for everyone in my family, regardless of what activities we were involved in.

Because Sundays were family days. For us, anyway.

All of our chores and homework had to be done before Sunday. We weren't allowed to go out with friends, but we were allowed to have friends over. If we left the house for an activity like cross-country skiing or a barbecue with the family across the street, whether it was a hike or a movie and pizza night, our family was together. Even at times when we were doing things separately—like reading, doing a puzzle, playing games—we were doing them together.

People often said, and still say, it was brave of my parents to keep me out of team practices—that it could have cost me my place on those teams. But my parents didn't see it as *brave*. They were just making choices based on their values. And they valued family. Now, I'm not saying that parents who let their kids practise with their teams on Sundays don't value family. But values are what help define our priorities, and our priorities are what guide us in our decision-making. And perhaps other parents just prioritized things differently. Perhaps they had other days of the week, or evening time, to spend as a family. As a physician and coroner in a somewhat rural community, my father worked long hours, including evenings and weekends. He was often called out by the RCMP to help with coroner's cases, and frequently made house calls to the homes of elderly people who couldn't make the drive into the office. (Yes, my dad still did/does house calls, like his father before him.)

Other people in my parents' situation might have different values and make different decisions, but as long as those priorities are as deeply rooted in their own values as my parents' decisions were, then they are the right choices. For them.

Some of life's choices really help shine a light on what you value most.

My parents made sure my coaches knew this rule in advance. They owned it as their decision, not mine. My parents told my coaches that they hoped this decision wouldn't be held against me, and that if my coaches needed to bench me, my parents would understand and take full responsibility.

But what if it had cost me? When people hear that story, they think about what the consequences might have been to me. But my parents thought about what the consequences would be to us as a family, and the consequences of not having the family time they valued and believed to be so important. It's true that my parents couldn't have cared less whether or not I pursued a career in sports. But that's not the point. The Family Day rule applied to *any* activity. My parents deeply valued time as a family. Their goal was to keep our family close. That was what mattered most to them, and so that's what guided their choices.

Now, there *were* rare exceptions to this rule. If there was a game on a Sunday or a tournament over the weekend (and *not* just a practice), and it did not conflict with something we had long planned to do, I could play in the game or tournament. My family would most likely be there to support me anyway.

I'm not going to say that, as a teenager, I *always* loved that Family Day rule. But my occasional resistance had nothing to do with me missing practices and everything to do with me not being allowed to watch the local Sunday night boys' hockey games with my girlfriends. Monday mornings my friends would be discussing the players from the night before, and I would feel left out. But my parents had the bigger picture in mind, and knew that a close family in the long run was more important than watching a boys' hockey game (or attending a sports practice). And I am grateful to them for their foresight and strength. They were in touch with their values, which helped clarify their priorities, which, in turn, made their choices easy for them. They chose authenticity and fulfillment as their definition of success.

I'm certainly not saying that what my parents did was easy, and perhaps you are doubting your inner strength and ability to create hard boundaries to protect the things most important to you, and stand up to the pressures of today's society. What about the parents who have to deal with coaches who say it *will* cost their child a spot on the field or any future in that sport? Or the employee who is told that he or she will have to work late to get in the boss's good books to be in line for a promotion? Or simply going with the flow and agreeing with the opinions of your friends *only* so you will not be shunned from a certain social circle?

What is *your* definition of success? Are you representing your authentic self? Do your outward accomplishments make you inwardly happy?

GUIDED BY PASSION

A few years ago, I ran into a gentleman at an event who, after an extensive discussion, passively commented on how he was still surprised that my brother had given up the opportunity to play volleyball for Canada. When I asked him what he meant, he explained that my brother had been recruited to play volleyball at Dalhousie University, being told that he could definitely play on the national team someday. My brother had turned down that opportunity, just as I had turned down bobsledding the first time they asked, so that he could play what he loved, which was basketball. Hearing that warmed my heart. He, too, obviously believed that reaching the top was—is—not fulfilling if your passion lies elsewhere. He played five years of varsity basketball at Acadia University in Nova Scotia, and then played a couple of years professionally in Switzerland. In hindsight, if you asked him about his decision, he would tell you he wouldn't have changed it for the world.

Just Because You *Can,* Doesn't Mean You *Should*

As I've mentioned, I was approached to try out for bobsledding *years* before I finally made the decision to compete in the 2005–06 season leading up to the Torino Olympics. When Dennis Barrett, the McGill University track coach acting as Bobsleigh Canada's Eastern Canada recruiter, told me in June 2001 that I had the perfect combination of strength and speed to be a world-class brakeman in the sport of bobsleigh, all I could think was, "What the . . . ? Who does *bobsledding*?" Despite Dennis's enthusiasm, I told him I just wasn't interested. After a brief pause, he continued as though I must not have heard him correctly, "But, Heather, you would be an *Olympian!*"

The excitement in his voice made it clear: He couldn't understand why anyone would not want to compete in the Olympics. Perhaps it had always been *his* dream. But, you see, at that time it was not mine. I was focused on my internship position as a Disability Sports Program Officer in Trinidad and Tobago through Commonwealth Games Canada, as it seemed that I had always wanted to work in a developing country. I hadn't grown up dreaming of bobsledding at the Olympic Games, but I *had* dreamed of working with people who, through no fault of their own, were born into less-than-desirable circumstances: people with disabilities; people in poverty; people who needed help in seeing the possibilities. To Dennis's complete bewilderment, I politely turned him down, and made the choice that was right for *me* at the time.

Why was I not swayed by the idea of becoming an Olympian? By being in the limelight? Because it hadn't been *my* dream. Why was I not swayed by the persuasion and arguments of others? Perhaps it was having grown up seeing the uncompromising integrity of my parents—making the choices that *they* believed were right for *them* and for our family, despite the pressures of society, the momentum of organized sports, or the fear of the unknown when taking the path less trodden. They weren't swayed by the opinions of other people. The views and judgments of others fell much further down their list of things of importance than the family values they had chosen.

Too often, we get caught up in other people's opinions, beliefs, and perceptions, not to mention their dreams. It's easy to get caught up in someone else's excitement over how *they* see the possibilities within an opportunity that you are presented with and therefore to overlook the possible consequences to you (both positive and negative) of a particular choice. But it is still *your* choice whether you pursue that opportunity or not. And not every opportunity is one worth pursuing—not because it doesn't offer good incentives but because it (or those incentives) may not align with *your* ultimate end goal or your values. Where will the choices take you? Which path will each option take you down? And what are your short-term versus long-term priorities?

Not every decision you face will be life-altering. But some will be forks in the road that will take some soul-searching in order to make the authentic choice for *you*. You often hear stories of someone who was presented with an opportunity they just couldn't refuse, usually implying a promotion, a raise in salary, a position of status and recognition, security. But . . . *could* they have refused it? Of course they could have. There is always a choice. And every choice comes with consequences. It is up to you to evaluate whether the good consequences outweigh the bad ones. Weighing the options with only successful outcomes in mind is much different than weighing the options with the undesirable outcomes in mind as well. Making an informed choice is about identifying and assessing the best-case *and* worst-case scenarios of *every* option, and making sure your final decision feels authentic to you.

Making Authentic Choices and Decisions

Shortly after the Sochi Olympics in 2014, I was offered the opportunity to work in a fairly prestigious position nationally, in a completely new industry for me. I was flattered that these nationally recognized people thought so much of me— that they believed I would be an amazing and effective person in that role, and that I could make a positive impact. They talked to me about the perks—big salary, crazy good pension, job security, status with the 'big-wigs'. But I was feeling extremely pressured—a sense of obligation that felt like a burden instead of an honour.

I always say that pressure is what we put on ourselves, what we internalize, and during that week of indecision I was feeling more pressure than I did at the Olympics. But deep down I knew I wanted to continue pursuing my new career as a motivational leader and speaker, which would mean an unpredictable income and little job security, but the chance to do what I love—motivating and empowering people all around the world. I knew in my heart that this is what I was meant to do.

So, after one of the most stressful weeks of my life, I politely turned the offer down. Sure, job security would be nice, but for me the pros did not outweigh the cons. I chose the path of authenticity and fulfillment over status, security, and money. Sometimes your decision may be based on the thing that's actually offered, and sometimes it may be more about timing. But that, too, must be taken into consideration. You need to respect where you are in your life. Priorities will shift over time, but they must still be considered. Sometimes we get overwhelmed with thinking that a certain opportunity won't present itself again. That may be true. But if it doesn't feel right for you at the time of your decision, then making any other decision wouldn't be authentic for you, at least not at that moment. And if the same opportunity *does* present itself again (like bobsledding did for me), simply re-evaluate the situation again. It *still* may not be the right choice for you. But . . . circumstances (and priorities) *may* have changed. It's all about *choosing your own adventure* and doing what's right for you, at the time that's right for you.

My father taught my siblings and me a process to help with decision-making. I think everyone knows the merits of simply listing and comparing the pros and cons of each choice. Well, my dad took it a step further. He added numeric values to each pro and con, allowing each option to end up with a final score that reflected how strongly you felt about it. For example, if you were considering moving to Calgary, distance from family might be a con, with a five out of five score, but accessibility to world-class training facilities would be a pro with a four out of five score. See how it works? At the end of listing and scoring everything based on fact *and* emotional and mental impact, you end up with a clearer picture, making decision-making much easier.

Heads or Tails

That being said, sometimes you are still left with a feeling of being torn—not knowing which of the two options is the best decision for you, and being paralyzed by not wanting to make the *wrong* decision (although there probably isn't a *wrong* decision, but just choices that lead down different paths). At this point, after having done my dad's authentic decision-making process, if you are *still* unsure, you can try this next suggestion. It is so effective and so simple, it is used in many different decision-making situations. It is what I call . . . *flipping a coin*.

You may think I'm joking, but I'm not. Once you have done a full analysis and have a clearer picture of everything that is involved with each choice, and you *still* cannot make a decision, then there is no harm in simply flipping a coin to help you decide. The key is that you must mentally commit to whatever choice the coin gives you. If you were *truly* being honest with yourself and, based on all pros and cons, you still had no preference, flipping a coin should solve the dilemma with whatever side the coin reveals. If, however, when the coin finally comes to a stop, lying flat on either its heads or tails side, you feel a sense of disappointment or sense of deflation, you have your decision. The *other* option is the right choice for you.

You may be thinking this is crazy, that anyone can just flip a coin and then change their minds, regardless of what side of the coin is showing. But the key is intention and commitment. Without commitment to the results of the coin flip, you will never get that gut reaction to tell you whether the coin's choice is right or wrong for you. It's not about the side of the coin that is showing, it's about what it *reveals* about how you are truly feeling about each option. It just may not have been clear before because of the perceived obstacles that that path will most likely present.

My sister-in-law, Allanna, was a physical education teacher and was starting to become frustrated with the education system and its bureaucracy and red tape. She wanted to have an impact but was finding it difficult to manoeuvre within the parameters of the system. She knew she wanted a change, and, knowing that I had become certified as an occupational therapist, asked me lots of questions about the program, the profession, and the options within that career path. She started looking into programs, but then suddenly an option to apply for funding became available for PE teachers, with the recipient being afforded the freedom to create and implement new programs for youth. The idea excited Allanna, but there were no guarantees that she would get the bursary, and also no guarantees that the funding would last more than a trial year. There was also a deadline to accept her spot in the occupational therapy program for which she had been accepted, and so she had to make a decision.

I was helping my aunt at her art gallery in Toronto when I suddenly got a phone call from Allanna, asking me to help her with her dilemma. Helping someone else with authentic decision-making is an art. To help someone come to a decision that is truly the right one for *them* requires that you listen carefully and not project your own feelings, fears, assumptions, or preferences on the other person or situation. A decision that may be right for one person may very well not be the right decision for the next person.

We talked for a while about her two choices. Finances were definitely part of the hesitation in changing career paths, as it would be for anyone—short-term struggle for long-term gain. But whenever she mentioned a pro about one choice, she would then follow it up with a con. It *seemed* as though the choices were evenly matched. So, I asked her if she did the pros and cons list, and she said that my brother had gone through the process with her, including the values, and, again, they *seemed* to be evenly matched. Then I asked her, "Do you really *not* have a preference? Are you leaning at all toward one choice more than the other?"

When she answered *no*, I asked, "So it really wouldn't matter which one you pursued then? It's just the difficulty of making the decision?"

When she answered *yes*, I bluntly stated, "Okay then, we'll just flip a coin." Her shock at simplifying this major decision to a coin flip was palpable through the phone, but when I reminded her that she said she really wasn't leaning toward one path more than the other, she reluctantly agreed.

I assigned each option to a particular side of the coin, and, figuratively, *flipped* it. *Teaching.* She would continue teaching and apply for the bursary, hoping to be able to create and implement her own programs in schools across Nova Scotia!

"Oh ... okay."

Those first words out of her mouth did *not* sound excited, nor did she sound relieved to have had the decision made. Which gave her the real answer she was looking for. And when I pointed that out, and the fact that it *was* only a 'coin flip' (that I hadn't actually done) and that she wasn't beholden to that result, she was so relieved. Allanna has been working as an occupational therapist since graduating in 2010.

HAVING WORKED WITH people with disabilities myself, and having gone through various work rotations throughout my master's degree in occupational therapy, I have witnessed and learned that there is more than one way to accomplish something, to reach a specified goal. Some people stay on a direct path, dealing with obstacles along the way; others choose a more scenic route, exploring different opportunities in life. There is more than one way to achieve your *way more*.

I have been told on a number of occasions that I am not normal, most often referring to the choices I've made along my path. I have been called the "anti-extremist elite athlete", having made choices contrary to what one would expect from a high-performance athlete. But what I found truly makes me unusual is not necessarily my willingness to make the unconventional choice but to do the 'abnormal' things because I *know* they are *right* for me and the people around me. The point isn't just that I was being unconventional for the sake of it but that my unconventional decisions were consistent with my goals, priorities, values, and beliefs at the time.

I am proud of the things I've accomplished so far in my life, but I am the *most* proud of having maintained my integrity and authenticity throughout my journey. And I learned that from my parents: Your priorities and values can guide you in your decision-making and lead to authentic choices that will lead to having no regrets. If you make choices that do not align with your values, you are never going to feel successful and fulfilled, no matter how many medals you earn, how much money you make, how many followers you have, or what floor your corner office is on. Those inauthentic choices will lead you *away* from fulfillment and the best version of yourself. That leads, at best, to *the hollow success of inauthenticity*: people with money and titles who feel like outsiders in their own lives because they strayed from their values and priorities.

Is success without fulfillment really success at all? Or is it just wealth? Or status? A prime parking spot and annual concert tickets? If you pursue anything without authenticity—even a gold medal race—you won't feel successful, despite achieving what looks like success to others.

Choose authenticity instead. Take the first step and ask yourself: What is important to me? What do I truly value? What different choice can I make tomorrow that supports those values and who I truly am, as well as my own goals for the future *I* want; not what *others* want, or who *they* want me to be?

Against the Grain

As I alluded to earlier, being authentic often goes hand in hand with making unconventional choices. Pursuing *your* dream and making the most of your potential can mean going against the grain, resisting pressure and even well-intentioned advice from other people to do what they think you should do, and taking a risk so that you can achieve your *way more*.

Because I did not grow up dreaming about going to the Olympics, I wasn't swayed by the historical and traditional actions of athletes, nor was I swayed by their decisions that were influenced by dreams of making the Olympic team. I made decisions that were right for me. I certainly wasn't a diva about it—I just made decisions that I knew deep down would ultimately help my performance and keep my sanity and my ability to achieve my goals. Sometimes that meant making difficult, unconventional choices, which often involved standing up to lots of external pressure.

> **"I am not a product of my circumstances. I am a product of my decisions."**
>
> **STEPHEN R. COVEY**

Standing Up for Yourself

It was certainly not a straight and easy path. After finishing my master's degree, I returned to the bobsled team in the fall of 2007 with the goal of standing on the podium in Vancouver 2010. At the time, I was still teamed up with Helen Upperton. Helen had landed a pretty big sponsor who was willing to invest in the team as a whole but was concerned about me playing rugby because of the injury risk. I sat down across from this very wealthy and influential businessman and was told that they (the sponsor group) wanted me to quit rugby until after the Vancouver Olympics. I told him I understood his concerns, but Bobsleigh Canada had recruited me as a rugby player, and I wasn't willing to give that up. I *loved* rugby. He started to explain the finances that they were willing to invest in the team as a whole—not just Helen—but that, unfortunately, playing rugby made me a high-risk investment. I have no idea where I found the assertiveness and the strength to respond the way I did, but through an emotional tightness in my throat, I said, "But... high risk, high reward."

The businessman just stared at me, then slowly cracked a smile (just a little one). There was nothing he could really say. I told him that if they thought I was too much of a risk, I would understand and would find my own way. For me, rugby was not negotiable.

As I have already emphasized, there are consequences to every choice. I had a great bobsleigh season that winter, and then in the spring of 2008 after the sliding season was over, I played in two international rugby sevens tournaments. The first one was in Hong Kong and the second was in Amsterdam, where I broke my shoulder. Although I was anticipating an "I told you so," I *still* did not regret my decision because I stayed true to who I was and what was important to me. But I *did* learn from the consequences, and chose not to play rugby the summer before the Vancouver Olympics, promising to rejoin the rugby team again for tryouts for the World Cup team right after the Olympics were over.

Being the Odd One Out

In the spring of 2010, following the Vancouver Games, a very reputable chiropractor told me that cold ice baths (taken by so many elite athletes for recovery) were not good for me. Apparently, I wasn't dealing with tight muscles like most athletes. I was dealing with tight fascia (the plastic-wrap-like casing that surrounds all muscle groups in the body). He suggested that I switch to warm Epsom salts baths. So, I did.

I rejoined the National Senior Women's Rugby Team only a couple months after the Vancouver Olympics for a training camp tryout followed by a game against the United States at the end of the week. Selections for the 2010 Rugby World Cup would be made based on this camp.

Let me tell you, it is not easy being the *only* one on a team doing something different. *All* of my teammates were taking scheduled cold ice baths after certain training sessions. And every time they would do ice baths, I would soak in a warm one. I knew the rest of my team was bonding by suffering together through the torture of submerging themselves in blow-up kiddie pools filled with freezing waters while I was off in some hotel bathroom. As much as I *hated* ice baths (and had been treated for hypothermia twice after such experiences in the past), it was still difficult to differentiate and isolate myself from the team. When you were a kid, do you remember hearing adults asking, "If all your friends jumped off a bridge, would you follow?" That's supposed to be a question that prompts some internal insight and aware-ness—about making your own decision based on what's right for you. But, although the automatic placating answer is, "No, of course not," unfortunately the real-life answer is... *probably*. Especially if there's anyone around to see. The fear of rejection—being left out—promotes a peer pressure that may or may not include the taunting of others. It's not easy to fol-low your own path when you just want to be... *included*.

But, as difficult as it was, I made the choice to do what I thought was best for my performance. And if Epsom salts baths would help me, then it meant they were also helping the team. I stayed strong and had the best season of my life.

How many times do you avoid making a conscious decision because it's easier to go with the flow? The choices that are right for you are often the hardest ones to make. But to fulfill your potential, you need to stand up for what is right for you— the choices that will lead to a life of fulfillment.

As it turned out, insisting on taking Epsom salts baths was not the only thing I had to stand up for.

Just Say No

I have had the pleasure of playing rugby in many different countries while representing Canada. I have also had the pleasure of playing rugby on various local teams while liv-ing and working not only in Canada but also in Ireland and Trinidad and Tobago.

I had just joined a particular team, and we were intensely preparing for an important upcoming game. (Yes, I am

intentionally making these details as vague as possible, as I
don't believe the identity of the people involved is important
to the story.) All the players received a schedule for game day,
which included a pre-game meeting to go over the game plan
and to take some kind of energy-boosting powder (or something like that). Having no idea what that meant, I asked the
trainer what it was and what was in it. He said it was "great
stuff" and "completely fine" and offered to give me a list of
the ingredients. I told him that unless it was third-party
tested and was officially approved as a safe and legal supplement for athletes, I wouldn't feel comfortable taking it. He
said he would send over all the information for me to take a
look at. Which he did. And which I did that evening.

The next day was game day, and I went with the other
players to the team meeting. I listened intently to the game
plan strategy that the coach had divided into quarters of the
game. And then the trainer told everyone to line up for their
drink mix. There were about twenty-five women there, all
lining up for their 'boost', which would supposedly kick in
just before kick-off. I just quietly sat in my chair, thinking
that no one would notice me in the midst of the organized
chaos in the room.

The trainer announced at the end of the meeting that he
wanted me to stay behind. He said that I had openly defied
him when, in fact, I simply sat quietly at my table *not* attract-
ing any attention whatsoever. He made me feel small and said
I was just trying to be difficult in front of the other players. I
hadn't say a *word*! He said that I should have told him ahead
of time. I reminded him of our conversation the day before,
and although the information he had sent seemed fine, it was
not a third-party tested supplement and I was in no way interested in taking the risk—an unnecessary one, in my opinion.
It was not worth it for me. If I ever took something that was

even unintentionally tainted by a banned substance, people would always question whether I had properly *earned* and *deserved* any of my former accomplishments. And I was not prepared to ever risk tarnishing my reputation as an athlete *or* as a person.

My opinion was (and still is) if I needed to take a supplement to be good enough to stay on the team, then maybe that meant I just wasn't good enough. And, if my own abilities weren't enough without external assistance, I was okay with not making the team.

The trainer was not happy. His final comment to me as I left was something to the effect of me not caring about my performance *or* the team. I walked back to the team cabins to prepare for the game, feeling pretty emotional. Feeling like I had just been bullied. Even though I had stood up to the pressure, it still shook my core.

I scored two of the three tries in that game. And as the whole team walked off the field, feeling excited about the big win, the trainer clapped me on the back with a big smile on his face and said, "Great job, Heather. I knew you could do it." Wow.

CONSCIOUS FUEL

I am very conscious of the things I put in my body. Not so much in terms of food (like salad versus candy—I like both), but more in terms of things that could, potentially, be tainted with a banned substance. It's not just whether the substance itself was meant to be performance-enhancing but that it may have been created in a laboratory where other substances may be, and tainting with trace amounts is possible. Even at well-known smoothie stands, I never 'boost' my juice with protein simply because I don't know where that protein has come from and whether it is 'safe' for athletes in terms of testing.

After the 2010 Vancouver Olympics, while I was training for the 2010 Rugby World Cup, I started drinking BioSteel ("Drink the Pink") during my training sessions. It wasn't until the fall of 2012 that I started using BioSteel's protein powder and recovery formula powder in my post-workout shakes. BioSteel was actually created by my trainer, Matt Nichol—one of the best people on the planet—and although he could have offered it to me earlier, he didn't even tell me it existed until it had gone through all of the procedures of third-party testing and approval by CCES (Canadian Centre for Ethics in Sport). This means that there is no risk of any batches being accidentally tainted by other banned substances. No stress. And actually delicious! (P.S. I was not paid to write this.)

'Pushing' for Goals

Although not unique to the sport of bobsleigh, or even sporting environments in general, the training atmosphere was, in a lot of ways, toxic: manipulation, small-p politics, walking on eggshells around certain people, trying to manage conflicting personalities within a small team who live in close quarters while travelling together for five months for the World Cup season. A total mind squeeze.

Don't get me wrong, there were some wonderful people in the sport, and some people with whom I miss spending time.

And some people thrive in that competitive, high-performance environment. I just found that dealing with the unfortunate mind games was much more exhausting and mentally painful than the physical exhaustion and pain of training for hours a day.

So, despite team expectations, I chose *not* to move to Calgary to train with the National Bobsleigh Team in a multimillion-dollar indoor push-training facility. To this day, I believe I am the only sliding athlete who never moved to Calgary (or did not, at least, live within driving distance to the training facility).

Athletes fly from countries all over the world and *pay* to train in that Ice House facility, and I chose *not* to have that at my disposal. I passed up the opportunity to train in an elite high-performance environment with amazing world-class technology!

I was fully aware that my efforts in training could potentially fall short by taking an unconventional, non-approved path; that I might not have been good enough to qualify for the team because I had chosen not to integrate myself into the team during the off-season. I knew that there would be consequences to my decision. And I was okay with that.

I had to make the choice that I believed was right for me; and I truly believed that, although unconventional, my choice to train closer to home in a much less stressful environment would allow my physical training to be more effective.

One of the coaches at the time told me that if I was really serious about winning a medal at the Olympics, I would move to Calgary. I looked at him with a confused smile on my face (and friendly twinkle in my eye) and said, "Really? I thought if I were serious about winning a medal at the Olympics I would train my ass off! I didn't realize it was about geography and I just had to move!" So I stayed home, training between Toronto and P.E.I. And decided to make it work for me.

Think about all the companies now that are allowing employees to work from home or allowing flex hours so they can work during the times of the day that are most productive to each individual. It is not about 'putting in the hours' and being *seen* putting in an effort (that kind of effort is often more about appearance than actual output); it is about productivity and results.

Choosing *not* to train in Calgary may have provided more challenges for my training, and I may have opened myself up to criticism, but that choice aligned with my priorities, and was truly the best decision for me! Being in what I considered to be a healthy environment for me also meant being reminded on a daily basis that there are things more important than sports. And going to a nephew's t-ball game after a long day of training was definitely a reminder of that (not to mention a de-stressor... as long as he was running in the right direction).

However, knowing it was the right thing for me didn't mean that it wasn't a difficult decision. In a way, I was making things more difficult for myself. And I didn't want to regret that decision. I didn't want that decision to be an *excuse* for me not training as hard as I needed to get the results that I wanted. But what could I do to compensate for giving up the opportunity to train in a high-performance environment with world-class equipment?

Well, with a shift in perspective, who's to say we don't have good technology in P.E.I.?! On every day that the training schedule said "push training in the Ice House", I pushed cars in a parking lot! (My brother likes to say that he helped with my training because he sat in the front seat of the car with the gear shift in neutral, windows down, blaring "Eye of the Tiger" from the radio while I pushed from behind!)

It doesn't matter where you come from when it comes to achieving success. I'm not saying that living in some places doesn't provide its own challenges, but blaming geography or lack of opportunity for not achieving your goals is just an excuse.

You can choose to see the limitations. Or you can *choose* to see the possibilities. When I was in P.E.I. for the Christmas holidays, I still needed to train, but it would have been unsafe to try pushing a car in the snow. Some people might have complained about the lack of indoor parking lots in such a small town, where they *could* have pushed their car for training. They could have simply given up on the idea of pushing a car, and used the lack of facilities as an excuse. But . . . I called the mayor—not someone often accessible to many people in bigger cities—and he helped me come up with a solution. I pushed a car for training in an empty potato warehouse down on the waterfront.

My choice? Unconventional. But no excuses. And it worked for me.

TIP **ADVICE FOR THE CAR LOT**

If you're in the market to buy a new car (and you live in a snowy climate), pushing a Chevy Malibu is a lot easier than pushing an Odyssey minivan, and Toyota Echoes are actually quite light! And, no, I've never been sponsored by a car company (*yet*). ☺

Mistakes Happen

Mistakes. Sometimes you make mistakes. Bad choices. You order the wrong meal, thinking it was something you'd actually like. (Yes, I have done this, which is why I generally order only meals I *know* I will like, or very plain-ish sounding meals at new restaurants.) You spend money on an online course you think will help increase the productivity of your business, but it turns out to be a flop. (Yes, this too, although I have also taken some great online courses.) You agree to go on a blind date. (Yep! I don't want to get into it.) You trip walking across the stage at graduation. (Fortunately, that has never happened to me, but now, as a professional speaker, I'm very wary of this. I did, however, trip getting out of the back of the bobsled at the end of a race, land and slide backwards on my bum, and *wave* into the camera that was in my face because we had finished third in that World Cup race. Along with thousands of people, my brother and his whole class were watching the race live online.) You say the wrong word. (The summer before my grade nine school year, I told the guy I had a crush on that he should have seen the jellyfish that had wrapped its testicles right around my leg! *Testicles!* "You mean, *tentacles*?" said the girl standing right beside us. Yep! I've *definitely* used the wrong word.)

We are all going to make mistakes, fall down, embarrass ourselves, but you can't let those missteps stop you from pushing forward. I'm not saying they shouldn't or won't *sting* at the time, but mistakes are simply mistakes. Mistakes happen. And the sting of mistakes goes away. Regrets, however, are a much bigger issue. Rooted in feelings of sadness, guilt, and disappointment, they linger in our minds.

Hindsight is 20/20, as the saying goes. It is only with the ability to reflect on past choices that you can feel regret—a lingering and often sinking realization that you should have done things differently. That you should have made a different choice along the way. You can only regret things you think you had control over—if you believe you could have changed the outcome, perhaps by making a different choice, trying harder...

I chose to miss the wedding of one of my best friends. It was in September 2009, during the pre-season of the Olympic year. Do I wish I could have gone? Absolutely. But do I regret not going? No. Had I gone and *not* done well that season, I would have always wondered whether that choice made the difference. As it is, I still get to visit with them all the time, only now as an Olympic champion. But a different choice, ending in a different outcome, would have *haunted* me. And *that* could have resulted in regret.

There are two different kinds of regret: the regret of actions right after they have happened—'I can't believe I said that'—or the regret of inactions—things you regret *not* doing. According to studies, people tend to regret things they *didn't* do more than things they *did* do. With *action regret*, we mentally punish ourselves right away, but as time passes, those mistakes don't tend to bother us as much. *Inaction regret,* however, often becomes clear only with time, leaving us with the sick feeling that something we chose *not* to do could or would have dramatically changed our life. We pine for the lost chance to change the current circumstance or situation, or to find greater fulfillment.

The things that people most often regret have to do with education, career, use of time, travel, health, and romantic relationships. Not spending as much time with your kids as you'd like because you are operating on the assumption that you *have* to work that many hours to improve the financial security of your family, only to one day realize that your kids are grown and you don't really know them. Not asking for advice or help that would advance your business because you want to appear confident and knowledgeable, only to be struggling in a home office, desperately holding on to a vision that you can't seem to get off the ground. Not living a healthier lifestyle, falsely assuming that *you* are too young for health issues to creep into your life, only to be faced with a medical wake-up call. Not following your passion and instead working in a profession that you believe will give you financial security, only to one day be laid off because of department restructuring. Not travelling because you believe you can't abandon your responsibilities, only to find yourself listening to the adventure stories of *others,* and feeling that you lack interesting experiences. Not putting money aside for retirement or a rainy day, only to be faced with that rainy day sooner than you had anticipated.

It's natural to contemplate different scenarios that *might* have been. I sometimes wonder what my life would be like had I taken sports more seriously when I was younger. Or had I pursued music instead of academics. Or had I said no to bobsledding *again.* But there's a difference between contemplating the past and dwelling on your choices with *regret.*

For some people, this kind of questioning can lead to the 'What if?' trap—the constant questioning of how their life would look if they had just made a different choice, taken a different path. *What if you had done [insert action] instead of what you actually did? What if you had chosen a different career path? What if you had had the courage to ask that person out on a date years ago? What if you had chosen to travel instead of enter straight into university? What if you had stood up for yourself against that bully in grade school? What if you had stopped smoking years ago when you promised yourself you would? What if you had accepted that job in a foreign country? What if you had worn something different to that interview? What if? What if?*

It can go on and on—your mind spinning in circles, questioning different choices you made in the past and comparing your current situation with the ideal one you created for yourself in your mind. This 'What if?' trap is very dangerous. It can suck you into depression and/or anxiety, thinking that, had you made a different choice somewhere along the way, your current life would, somehow, be better. It makes you think of only the negative things in your current life, and not the positive things. Yes, a different life choice would have led to a different life, but there's nothing to say it would have been better. Just different. Things may even have turned out to be worse, had you made a different choice.

I HAVE BEEN asked a number of times if I wished I had started training and pursuing the Olympics when I was younger, how many Olympic Games I think I could have competed in had I started earlier, how many sports I could have competed in at the international level had I taken sports seriously at a younger age.

Although it's hard sometimes not to wonder "What if?" I am grateful that my athletic life transpired as it did. Starting that level of training and focus as an older athlete, I had a very different perspective that allowed me to see different options and solutions than I believe I would have seen otherwise. I was less inclined to be swayed by the norm—by what all the other athletes were doing—and pressured into making choices that weren't authentically best suited for me and what I wanted for my life.

I have met too many athletes who don't seem to have had a childhood, who have put all of their energy and focus into being the best in the world. But at what cost? Often athletes put everything on hold to chase a moment, and then it's gone. The thing is, you can't put your childhood on hold. It's something that, as much as you try, you can't get back.

Sometimes athletes are so driven and focused on one goal, they don't realize that it's not what they *really* want. Or they get caught up in the process, and can't remember why they originally chose that path (or if it was a conscious choice to begin with). Sometimes athletes are so driven and focused on achieving one particular outcome that they are too scared to miss a training camp or tour (which sometimes costs amateur athletes or their parents thousands of dollars) in fear that someone else might take their spot and they might not get selected for the next big event.

In the end, you must know you can make unconventional choices and still succeed on the same stage as others and be part of the team. As I learned from high school, going with the flow may not be the way to achieving your highest level of success and fulfillment. Going with the flow may not be the way to realizing your potential.

As I mentioned, there are consequences to lying—and there are consequences to lying to ourselves. When you make an excuse, or make a choice that is not right for you, you get 'busted' by the results: falling short of your goals or not feeling fulfilled. The result is regret, knowing deep down that you could have done things differently to change the outcome had you just done it *your* way.

10

PLAN

Turn Big Dreams
into Big Action

B Y NOW YOU should be able to see that to feel fulfilled in your life, you need to make the choices that are right for you—the ones that align with your values, the ones that infuse you with inner satisfaction instead of simply giving you the means to afford external *stuff*—and pursue the goal that makes you the happiest.

You should also be realizing that you are capable of *way more* than you are currently giving yourself credit for. But, you may be wondering, how do you make it happen? How do you actually take the path to your *way more*?

Have you ever wondered what makes someone successful? Have you ever wondered how a peer or colleague became successful when they didn't seem to be any more outwardly skilled at his or her job than anyone else?

On the flip side, how many of your peers throughout school who seemed to be extremely skilled, possibly even gifted, in a particular area—arts, sciences, music, sports— never reached the top levels of performance within their respective fields? How often have you recalled someone you've met in the past and thought they totally wasted their talent, thinking they had been capable of doing so much more with their life?

Why does that happen? Why do some people with no apparent natural gift reach a level of high performance while others, who seemed naturally gifted from birth, never come close to realizing what everyone else saw as their potential?

Although you do need to develop specific skills to perform certain activities, personality traits and characteristics actually make the difference. Some people try to attribute my success in sports to my athletic giftedness. But that's not all it is. Had I not made the *choice* to pursue sports seriously at the highest levels, I would have been working as an occupational therapist with the same amount of athletic *giftedness* or potential—it just would have been untapped, and I never would have discovered the extent of what I could accomplish athletically. Yes, I may be more gifted athletically than the general population, but it took other things to help me realize my full potential in three different sports—things like an external catalyst, an optimistic attitude, support from others, and mental toughness.

When some people hear what I've accomplished athletically, they almost explain it away by saying that I'm naturally gifted—that I have an athletic gene. But that alone didn't make me a champion. Nobody is born a champion, just like nobody is born a CEO! Yes, genetic advantage is real and it makes a difference. But having a genetic advantage simply means that you have more potential than others in a certain area. Potential, if untapped, will not beat a growth mindset and hard work. And not having as much potential as others doesn't block you from doing whatever it is you want to do. You can still be good at something without being naturally talented in that particular thing, it just might be a little more difficult for you.

What are your strengths? What is your passion? And what is it going to take to turn your dreams into reality?

Dream Big

Dreaming big is the first step to making your life the best it can be. Dreaming allows you to see and define the things you want in life—what you want it to look like and how you want to feel. This is why many experts talk about creating personal vision boards with words and images depicting what you want in your future. But dreaming big is not enough! You cannot tap into your potential simply by dreaming.

Many people feel as if they are wandering aimlessly in the world without purpose. They work hard at what they do but are simply going through the required day-to-day motions and, hence, don't seem to get very far. They are living a life without a sense of fulfillment. For most of those people, a fundamental reason for this directionless living is that they haven't stopped what they are doing long enough to spend time thinking about where exactly they *want* to go—what they *want* to get out of life. Most thoughts of a better, let alone ideal, life are often dismissed before any consideration is even given to the possibilities of achieving it. It's hard— pretty much impossible—to set your actionable compass on a path to a desired life destination if you don't know where you want to end up. It cannot happen without clear, specific goals. It's hard to know what to do when you don't have a plan, and goals bring clarity to a vision.

So, what is the difference between a goal and a dream? A dream (or vision) is something you think about and *wish* could be a reality of your life. It is a passive hope. A goal, on the other hand, is something you plan to achieve and then actively pursue. I once drove by a church billboard that read, "Wishing and wanting is different than pursuing." Wanting to date someone, for example, is very different than starting a conversation with that person, sending him or her flowers or a note, actually asking them out. Wishing and wanting stays in your mind. Pursuing goals means taking action.

Dreaming big is not enough!

Define Success

The process of setting goals means first figuring out what is important to you, choosing what you want your future to look like, and *then* determining how to get there—how to turn that vision of what your future *could* be into your very own reality. But sometimes knowing what you want to achieve is half the battle. Companies, for example, have mission and vision statements that keep employees focused on the ultimate direction and goal of the organization, guiding their decisions and actions. Mission and vision statements have become a vital aspect of success for organizations, so why don't we, personally, have them too? Statements that clearly define a vision of what we want our future to look like, what we want to achieve, and what we stand for.

There are as many definitions of success as there are people on this planet because it is such a subjective and personal thing, so it is important to spend the time developing *your* definition of success. Without this clarity, you won't know what you are working toward. You may be working toward a work-life balance so you can be at home more with your children. Or you may be working toward the goal of eventually selling your start-up. *I* didn't just train for general strength and fitness when I was pursuing my Olympic goals; I was training specifically for bobsledding. Meaning, I didn't have to build up my cardio at all—I only had to have explosive power and speed for no more than six seconds (which *did* make things challenging for me when transitioning from bobsledding to rugby season for which I *did* need to have more cardio). I didn't train just to build strength—to lift as much weight as I could. I trained to lift as much weight as I could as *quickly* and as *explosively* as I could. (I could be stronger than anyone, but if I couldn't move that weight *faster* than others, it wouldn't matter.)

It is also important to prioritize your goals if you have more than one, so that if you are faced with conflicting goals, you will already know which one comes first, which one is most important to you. For example, you may have one goal of completing a master's degree or a particular project in two years but may prioritize quality time with your family above that goal, which means that if something family-related comes up within those two years that needs your attention, you won't have to think twice about where your time will be spent. Achieving your goal of getting a promotion in two years may not be *as* important as spending time with family.

"No matter how talented you are, it's the choices you make that will really determine whether you tap your potential in a positive way."

JOHN C. MAXWELL

Believe in Your Path

As I mentioned, a number of obstacles to achieving your goals can pop up during your pursuit—real or perceived obstacles that have to be overcome in order to continue along your path. But what stands in the way of people even turning their dreams into goals in the first place? Why don't they even *try*? I believe there are two main obstacles at this initial stage: the lack of belief that achieving the desired goal is at all possible and comfort.

Belief is extremely powerful, as I've discussed earlier in the book, and without it—without believing in the possibilities— you will limit what you can achieve and your life will feel less than fulfilled, like something is missing. Without the *belief* that a desired outcome is, in fact, a possibility, however, why bother pursuing it in the first place? Why make it a goal at all?

The wrong perspective can hold you back from so many things, and not believing in the possibilities can stop you before you even start. For example, if you believe that genetics and natural talent are the most essential ingredients to success, you've created your own obstacle if you don't think you're as blessed with those gifts as other people. You must learn to see talent as a skill that can be learned and developed. And when you shift to that perspective, you will see that passion can get you closer to accomplishing your goal by believing in the possibilities and having perseverance and resiliency.

You want to be successful at something? Stop making excuses and holding yourself back by staying in your comfort zone. It's time to change your mindset to believe in the possibilities and be willing to feel a bit uncomfortable.

Step Outside the Comfort Zone

Let me share a fundamental truth: I would never have discovered that I was capable of winning two Olympic gold medals had I not overcome the anxiety brought on by just the *thought* of ... wearing a full spandex suit in front of millions of people!

I remember my first bobsleigh race in November 2005, and it felt *horrible*. Not because of the weather or the result but because of the *thinnest* of material suctioned to my body, with nothing underneath except for underwear and a *burn vest* in the event of a *crash*!

That may not seem like a big deal to you, but for me it was almost a deal-breaker. I mean, when I grew up it was trendy to wear your dad's baggy sweaters to school. Shapeless was trendy. So the idea of wearing a speedsuit was as uncomfortable as ... Well, let's just say I felt exposed.

But I've since realized that sometimes that's what needs to happen—that's how you need to feel—to take your life to the next level and discover what you are truly capable of. So, if you want to experience real change and get big results, you have to be willing to feel uncomfortable, whether it comes from physical effort, from having to make hard choices, or from feeling exposed. Which is another way of saying don't be afraid to be vulnerable. You might *feel* naked at first, but there is power beyond that exposure. For me, it was the first ride to a place I'd never even dreamed of being.

I know it's hard. Comfortable choices are so much easier. Comfort feels good, like wearing your dad's baggy sweater. For some, discomfort may simply mean the physical and mental exhaustion from practising and perfecting a new skill or the anxiety of appearing inexperienced.

But nothing of great significance happens when we wrap ourselves in comfort 24/7. Sure, you can perform successfully in your comfort zone. But being comfortable all the time mostly leads to complacency. And complacency never leads to high performance. When you play it safe, you prevent yourself from moving forward significantly in business, sports, or other aspects of life. You prevent yourself from discovering and fulfilling your potential.

You see, most of us set safe-ish goals for ourselves—goals that may move us forward but that are predictably achievable with only a few minor adjustments, requiring just a bit more of what we are already doing. I think I know what you're thinking: *It's not worth risking everything—status, social network, current income, autonomy—for an unsure outcome.* And let me be clear: there is nothing wrong with that way of thinking. *Any* kind of personal development and growth is commendable. But what if there *is* an outcome that is worth the risk? What if the *possibility* of an outcome is worth the risk?

"The greater danger for most of us is not that our aim is too high and we miss it, but that it is too low and we reach it."

UNKNOWN

We often wish and want for bigger and better things or for transformational change in our life. But are you willing to step outside of your comfort zone to make that happen? Risk feeling like a rookie again? Are there things you could be doing right outside your comfort zone that would move you closer to your desired outcome?

My willingness to feel uncomfortable in that moment before my first race (and for every race to come) was critical for me to reach the top of the Olympic podium. Not physical strength or stamina—that was the easier stuff for me—but the *willingness* to embrace *discomfort*. Had I not stepped outside of my comfort zone, whatever talent and skill I had would have remained unused—my potential untapped, and the possibilities of what I was capable of un-pursued. That same willingness is essential for everyone to maximize their potential and get to the next level, and to the *highest* levels in whatever arena of performance they choose.

A Case Study in Discomfort

In January 2016, I climbed the highest mountain in Antarctica with a group of people to bring awareness to the issues of post-traumatic stress disorder (PTSD) and to raise money to help our war veterans successfully reintegrate into civilian life after they've finished service. This expedition was organized by the True Patriot Love Foundation, a national charity that honours the sacrifices of members of the Canadian Armed Forces, and the group consisted of seven soldiers, sixteen civilians (mostly corporate people and me), three specialists (doctor, researcher, and photographer), and six guides, creating a team of thirty-two people.

A NOTE ABOUT PTSD

A recent movement has been lobbying to change the term *post-traumatic stress disorder* (PTSD) to *post-traumatic stress injury* (PTSI). Although the PTSD diagnosis (used since 1980) has helped to better identify what was once known as shell shock (among other names)—and has allowed for research into its causes, symptoms, and treatments—critics now say the word *disorder* carries a heavy stigma and prevents people from seeking help, especially those who have served in the military. Advocates suggest that changing *disorder* to *injury* helps to reframe the condition in a positive way and to focus on the possibility of rehabilitation and healing. PTSI diagnosis is considered to be more accurate, hopeful, and honourable. Around the year 2000, the Canadian military started using the term *operational stress injury* (OSI) within its community to acknowledge this condition as a work-related injury—an injury that occurred on the job. PTSI, however, is starting to gain more traction among the general public, as it also encompasses traumatic events that *don't* happen in the workplace.

It was a great cause, but what was I thinking? As far as I could tell, there were at least seven really good reasons for *not* accepting the challenge of climbing that mountain—seven uncomfortable things I realized I would have to struggle through if I accepted the challenge:

1   It's Antarctica, so it's cold! (Despite being Canadian and a Winter Olympian, I don't do well in the cold.)

2   It involves trekking for hours on end. (This is of no interest to me, as a sprinter, who doesn't even enjoy *walking* for exercise. So imagine my excitement at the thought of having to train by walking on a treadmill wearing a weighted backpack, let alone walking for hours on the side of a mountain.)

3 My mountain climbing experience is lacking. (And by 'lacking', I mean 'non-existent'.)

4 It's Antarctica, so it's cold!

5 I would have to deal with uncomfortable toileting practices. (By 'uncomfortable', I mean pooping in a bag like they do in the military, peeing in a bottle, or squatting over a seemingly bottomless hole that descended into the abyss of the mountain while completely exposed to the elements. They definitely don't show you *that* in the movies!)

6 It would be *so* exhausting at such a high altitude.

7 Did I mention, it's *Antarctica*? So it's *really freakin' cold*!

But let's take a step back for a second. What if we *come from away* and look at it from a different point of view? What if we shift our perspective? Instead of looking at only the uncomfortable reasons for *not* climbing the mountain, what, if any, would be the reasons *for* climbing that mountain?

A fantastic cause (but one to which I simply *could* have just sent a donation)! Or delivered a speech at one of their fundraisers. Or been the group's welcoming committee when they returned home... To be perfectly frank, when I first got the call and the guy on the other end of the line started explaining the charity and the expedition, I thought he was going to ask me to donate an autographed item to help raise funds at an auction. Not take on one of the most physically and mentally challenging (not to mention *coldest)* things I've ever done.

But I chose to go. Not without taking a few days to weigh the pros and cons, however. But it didn't take me long to realize that the only reason that I am able to live the life I choose to live is because the servicemen and -women of our Canadian Armed Forces *choose* to put their lives on the line for me, *choose* to fight for the freedoms that I take for granted on a daily basis, are doing a necessary job that I feel fortunate that I don't have to do.

This was also another opportunity for me to walk the talk. I mean, I speak to audiences and work with individuals, encouraging them to step outside of their comfort zones to discover what they are truly capable of, and, well, minus forty degrees Celsius would surely be out of *my* comfort zone. So, really, why shouldn't I?

Fear of *Uncomfortable* Failure

Risking failure is, to some, not just stepping but *leaping* outside of their comfort zones. Nobody really *wants* to fail. But it is actually not the failure itself that people fear but what he or she believes failure will bring, such as ridicule or rejection. To many people, it is much better to stay in a safe, comfortable place where they are accepted.

But discovering and living to your full potential is all about shifting your perspective to embrace the possibility of failure—the possibility of crashing—as a stepping stone to success, to take a step into the unknown—to pursue a goal without a guaranteed outcome, a goal with the risk of failure. You might be tempted to stay in a comfortable and relatively predictable goal-setting zone of performance, whether it be in sports, business, or relationships, but remember—nobody pays for average.

So, think really hard and try to see the potential that exists. *Believe* in the possibilities that lie beyond that limiting comfort barrier. Magical moments and newsworthy achievements don't happen in the predictable comfort zone. So, again, when you believe in the possibilities of what you *could* achieve, it comes down to a choice: comfort or magic.

Embrace challenges that sit at the edge of what you believe to be possible, and discover the extent of your potential.

Create an Action Plan

Setting goals is critical if you want to move toward your ideal life or the best version of yourself. Having a goal puts a spring in your step, gives you a sense of direction, a purpose. However, *if* you think your life is perfect—you are completely happy with everything about your life, feel a total sense of fulfillment, and wouldn't change a thing—then you may find no reason to set goals. But if you see any room for improvement, have any bucket list adventures in the back of your mind, want to learn new things, or just have the feeling that *something is missing*, then you need to introduce a goal into your life.

But how often do your dreams seem so big and 'far-fetched' that you never even *consider* that they could become a reality? How often do you not even give them a chance? Well, give yourself the freedom to dream big, to see what magic you can make in your own life. And allow yourself to believe in the possibilities. Turning a dream into a goal simply means you believe in the possibilities and are ready to take action toward achieving your desired outcome.

How do you transform your dream into reality? Well, a goal is simply a dream with an action plan. You must identify the outcome you want and then define smaller goals (a checklist of steps or milestones) that are essential to reaching your desired destination or achieving your desired result, whether that means becoming the CEO of a major corporate enterprise, moving into your dream home, travelling around the world, or spending more quality time with your family. For even more effectiveness, you should include a timeframe or deadlines for when each step and milestone will be achieved. Deadlines will promote action. Your goal will seem more attainable because you can visualize not only what you want but also the path to it and the specific steps that need to be taken to get there.

I know it sounds counter-intuitive, but to reach the highest levels of human achievement, you must turn your focus *away* from your goal and desired outcome. That's how to keep the possibly daunting nature of a goal at bay: Focus on the execution of each *individual step* that must happen for your dream to become a reality, and never let the 'highly unlikely' aspect of achieving what's possible cause you or your team to stray from that focus or the actual execution of a particular step. That is what needs to happen when pursuing *any* goal in sports, business, relationships, and life. It is about the process! It is about perspective, and being able to see the individual pieces that are really important—the individual building blocks—instead of being overwhelmed by that big picture.

I GAINED GREAT wisdom in climbing Mount Vinson—the most *literal* of analogies for breaking big goals down into manageable steps. When you climb a mountain, you can't allow yourself to get distracted from the path and let your eyes or your mind wander. If you get distracted on a climb, one of three things will most likely happen:

1   You will trip and stumble.

2   You will get sidetracked, stepping off the path into softer snow (making it more difficult for yourself, requiring more time and energy).

3   You will step on the rope attaching you to the person in front of you, causing that person to be halted in their progress and, therefore, decrease the efficiency of the entire rope team!

Did any of those things happen to me when I summited Mount Vinson? Of course they did! You may never battle the cold and the wind to summit a mountain. You will *likely* never have to recover from hip surgery in time to get back into a rugby jersey or a speedsuit to try to win a medal for your country. But in facing the challenges you face, you, too, need to focus on the process—one step at a time. Believe in yourself and the people around you! But:

Understand that you are going to make mistakes and trip and fall.

Understand that you are going to get distracted and step in 'soft snow'.

Understand that you are going to annoy someone because you step on his or her rope.

But also understand that incredible things are possible, that achieving success—your summit, your podium—is a process.

Don't let the fear of tripping stop you from pursuing your goal in the first place! And remember, you'll get stronger and more accomplished with every step you take along the way.

There are many books specifically about goal-setting, so I'm not going to go into a great deal of depth here. My point is to highlight the importance of knowing *where* you want to end up, clearly knowing what it's going to take to get there, and keeping things in perspective by focusing on one step at a time instead of being overwhelmed with the big picture.

These are the steps you need to take to move yourself toward your ideal life:

1 A dream or a vision

2 A specific goal

3 An action plan outlining the milestones to achieving that goal

4 Deadlines (timeframe) for achieving each milestone

5 Accountability (not essential, but it increases the likelihood of staying on target and making deadlines. Tip: Having an accountability partner—someone who will keep you honest with your commitments—will help you stay on track and move you toward your milestones and end goal.)

> **'Wanting and wishing' is very different from 'planning and pursuing'. One requires only thought, while the other requires action.**

KAILLIE HUMPHRIES AND I reached the top of the podium in Vancouver *and* Sochi because we were able to ignore the magnitude of what we were trying to do, and of what the Olympics mean, and focus on the checklist of specific things that had to be done. And that is what I'm doing right now as I attack the challenge of writing this book. As daunting as it seems to me, seeing as it is out of my 'wheelhouse' and I am basically a rookie again, I keep reminding myself to focus on the individual steps of the process: figuring out the overall message I want to convey; identifying the various topics that would help relay that overall message; recalling stories and personal experiences that would help convey those topics; writing one section at a time (one paragraph at a time, one sentence, one word); finding an editor; working step by step through the material; and so on.

Once you establish your goal and the steps to achieving that goal, you will get clarity on where to focus your efforts. This will also help you recognize and manage distractions. How often do we look up something specific on the Internet and then get distracted by a 'news' headline popping up (and, yes, I use the word *news* loosely), with an easily clickable link, that then leads us to another interesting story or a cute picture that looks like it leads to an interesting video? Goal-setting helps us to organize and manage our time and our resources more effectively; with a milestone *and* a deadline to reach that milestone, we are more apt to stay focused on getting it done.

But many people don't set goals (or only set very small goals) because they are overwhelmed by the big picture. So break it down. Not in a dancing kind of way, but in an in-depth analysis of the resources you need and the steps that need to happen to reach the finish line—whatever that end goal is for you.

Consider what a friend of mine told me about the coach of a junior hockey team that was losing 2-0 heading into the third period at a big tournament. He heard the players talking about how they had only one period to score two goals to tie. The coach knew he needed to make his players see the situation in a different way to even give them a shot of making a comeback possible, so he got their attention and told them what the *real* situation was:

"Guys, we don't have to score two goals! We just have to score one goal! Two times."

That coach broke it down, and, in doing so, put the situation in perspective for his athletes. He knew how overwhelming it can be when you can see only the big picture without breaking it down into the steps required to get there. He kept the possibility of winning in sight, and made it seem not nearly as dire or implausible to achieve that 'highly unlikely' objective simply by changing his team's *perception* of the situation. A shift in perspective can be enough to change your attitude, reassess your thinking, and question your assumptions, drawing your focus to what you need to do to turn even a highly unlikely outcome into a possibility. Experience tells you only what happened before; but history does not tell you what *could* happen—what's *possible* in the future.

Is It Worth It?

Once you break down your goal into steps, and you can see everything that will be involved in achieving your goal, you have a very important question to ask yourself: *Is it worth it?* If success is guaranteed, perhaps. But there *are* no guarantees. Sooo . . . Is what is involved in the *pursuit* of your goal worth it, regardless of whether you succeed or not? Sometimes the answer is, in fact, no. And that's okay. That is very authentic self-awareness, and pursuing it anyway would lead you further from fulfillment. So, is it worth it?

A few years ago, I read a great article exactly about that very topic: Mark Manson's "The Most Important Question of Your Life." Manson writes about how everyone wants to be financially independent, work in one's dream job, be super healthy and fit, have an amazing relationship and great sex. Nothing about that is unusual. But what is unusual, unfortunately, is that that scenario is not as often a reality as one would hope. Why not? Well, Manson puts it all into a brilliant perspective by saying that instead of asking people what they want out of life, the better question to be asked is: "What pain do you want in your life? What are you willing to struggle for? Because that seems to be a greater determinant of how our lives turn out."

What's *your* goal? What is involved in achieving that goal? Are you willing to suffer through sixty-hour work weeks? Are you willing to wake up extra early to go to the gym before work? Are you willing to miss family events and vacations and long weekends? Are you willing to have tough conversations? I attended a seminar in 2015 and heard John C. Maxwell say, "People always say they want to do what I do. But are they willing to do what I did?"

Answering those questions is not made easier simply by knowing the tangible or visible outcomes—the corner office on the forty-sixth floor, the qualification for a national sports team, or getting a parent-of-the-year award—superficial goals to satisfy your ultimate (and often unidentified) goal of achieving a certain feeling. What *feeling* are your striving for? Your *root why* is about what that outcome does for you—your sense of self-worth, your need for security, validation, and so on. Those feelings—your *root why*—will help you determine whether an outcome is *worth struggling for.*

"Behind every great achievement is a story of education, training, practice, discipline, and sacrifice. You have to be willing to pay the price."

JACK CANFIELD

THE GOAL OF IMPROVEMENT

One of my nieces had recently turned five when I was visiting her and my brother's family just outside Halifax, Nova Scotia. She had been taking skating lessons for the winter and was so excited (as was I) that I would get to see her skate during one of her lessons.

I watched with a heart about to burst as she cautiously manoeuvred across the ice—literally inch by inch. She fell a number of times but managed to get back up with a combination of focus and then delight and pride on her face. And the smile that beamed out from under her helmet when aimed toward those of us watching warmed my heart even more (if that's even possible).

When the lesson was over and she made her way off the ice, I exclaimed how happy I was to have seen her skate. I told her that I knew how tough learning something new could be, but it looked like she was working really hard to get better. She happily and matter-of-factly replied, "Well, Auntie, you have to start somewhere!"

That evening, we Skyped with her mother, who was away for a meeting. When asked how skating went, my niece proudly and excitingly said, "Mommy, I am getting so much better! This time I spent more time on my skates than on the ice!"

If only we could all take some of that perspective to move us forward when trying something new, even if only by an inch at a time.

Understand the *Root Why*

How do you figure out your *root why*? Well, purpose is the reason behind taking a particular action. Motivation is what drives action. These two concepts are intertwined, as your

How often do your dreams seem so big and 'far-fetched' that you never even *consider* they could become a reality?

purpose serves as your motivation. But more often than not, people will act without knowing their purpose—the reason *why* they are acting. Or if they *do* think they know the reason why they are doing something or pursuing a particular outcome, it is often a superficial *one.*

I get asked questions about motivation quite frequently (Olympic athletes tend to know a thing or two about that). I have even worked with individuals struggling with this in their lives, including a lawyer who was grappling with motivation in his work. People want to know how to stay motivated when in pursuit of reaching their goals. The key to motivation is having a sense of purpose. And I believe you need to dig deep to get to the *real* one.

A purpose helps clarify your goals. Or, more specifically, a purpose provides a *reason* for achieving your goals because sometimes having a dream is not enough. In fact, it is not often achieving the goal itself that is the purpose for pursuing it; it is what the achievement of that goal will bring. For example, two people could be pursuing the same goal of losing a certain amount of weight. Person 1's stated motivation (or reason *why*) could be to look good at an upcoming high-school reunion or on the beach in the fast-approaching summer. Person 2's reason *why* could be motivated by health concerns following a recent scare with a family member.

But for each of them to get to their *root why*, the question *why* needs to be asked again and again until they know the *real* reason. For Person 1, the deep-seated purpose may be a need for recognition or a sense of validation. For Person 2, it may be to live longer to be able to spend more time with grandkids, prompted by a health scare. Different people may have the same goal, and maybe even the same first-level *why*, but knowing the *root why* will help each of them stay motivated when times get tough. And sometimes thinking about the repercussions of *not* reaching your goal is an even bigger and more powerful motivation than imagining yourself having achieved all your goals.

Simon Sinek is a well-known author and TED Talks speaker, known for his book and keynote *Start with Why*. Sinek talks about how the highly successful companies are those which focus their marketing on the *why* of the organization, inspiring people to buy into what the company believes in—what it stands for—with buying the actual product being a secondary result: "People don't buy *what* you do; they buy *why* you do it." They get inspired by the *why*—the *reason*—for doing what you do. He informs his audiences and his readers that the *why* talks directly to the part of the brain that controls behaviour—the limbic system—and that we rationalize it with the tangible things we say and do—the *what*. Sinek explains that the limbic system is responsible for our feelings, behaviour and decision-making, relying on emotion and inspiration, and is where gut decisions are made. You can be faced with all the facts and figures to support a decision, but it still might not *feel* right.

But Sinek is referring to businesses, and how entrepreneurs can use their *why*—their reason for starting their businesses—to market in a better way to reach the people they want to reach—consumers who believe in what they believe in, who stand for what their company stands for—to build their success.

And all that makes sense. But I want to make it personal *and* go a step further: What is *your* why? Why do *you* do what you do? Why are you doing that particular job, in that particular industry? Why do you choose to do the things you do, and to pursue some of your goals over others? And I don't want the first superficial answer that comes to mind but your fourth or fifth level of *why* (if that's what it takes to get there)—your *root why*.

What do I mean by that? Well, when you answer your *why* question, ask the question again and again, like a curious five-year-old child, until you can't ask it anymore: "Why do I do what I do?" "Well, why is *that* important to me?" "And why does *that* matter to me?" And so on.

For example, money may be a strong motivator for you, but it may not be your *root why*. Sinek points out in his talk that money is a profit—a result—and that your *why* is your purpose, your cause, your belief. Does what you do align with your purpose? Your cause? Your belief?

Let's use another example—an extremely oversimplified example, doing laundry—to illustrate how you can get to your *root why*. Not many people can say honestly that they *love* doing laundry. It is usually a task scribbled somewhere on a to-do list, or a weekly scheduled chore, or something that we are simply reminded of when searching for something clean to wear. And sometimes that first-level why is not enough of a reason to keep us going.

But what about the second-level why? Or the third-level why? What about the *root why*?

Let me explain. Laundry. How many times do you hear someone say they *have* to do laundry? How often do you hear *yourself* saying it? *Having* to do laundry implies that you don't have a choice. But, although it may not *seem* like a choice, and you may not have any clean clothes to wear, you are still left with a choice: doing laundry and having clean clothes to wear *or* simply wearing dirty clothes. Now, if you live in your parents' basement and work from home, perhaps wearing clean clothes is not a priority, and wearing dirty clothes won't have any life-altering consequences. But if you work in an environment where you meet other people, whether you live in your parents' basement or not, wearing dirty clothes and therefore doing laundry or not *can* have consequences. Could you appear to be irresponsible? Could you be fired from your job?

Think about it in terms of your *why*. *Why* would you *want* to do laundry? To have clean clothes. *Why* do you care about wearing clean clothes? To make a good impression at work. *Why* do you want to make a good impression at work? To appear responsible and possibly get a promotion. *Why* do you care if you get a promotion? Because you want to make a good salary. *Why* do you care about making a good salary—more than you make now? Because you want your kids to be able to go to university. *Why* do you care if your kids go to university? Because you want them to have the benefits of a good education, which will give them options down the road. And *why* does *that* matter? Because you will feel fulfilled and successful, knowing that you raised successful kids.

So *why* do you want to do laundry? So that your children will have the benefits of a good education and will, ultimately, be happy because they have options. So that you will feel validated as a parent. Does that make laundry seem so daunting anymore? Geez, why didn't you say so sooner?

I didn't have more than a first- or second-level why in grade school or university. I did my homework because I wanted to pass the class and, ultimately, graduate and go to university. But beyond that, I had no idea what I wanted to *be* when I 'grew up', so I didn't really have any direction *at* university. I played sports—lots of sports—because I was naturally good at them and it was a social outlet. I had no passion, at the time, for trying to reach a higher level of competition. No underlying sense of purpose. I mean, they were only sports. I played only because I loved playing. There was no far-sighted vision of what being involved in sports *could* mean to me because I had no real *why*. I knew *what* I was doing, but without a deeper-level *why*, there was no reason or drive to move forward to a higher level, to push myself to see what I was truly capable of.

I really admire young people who seem to have discovered their passion and their purpose at an early age—who have figured out their *why*, not only their *what*. I recently spoke at a women's empowerment event in Toronto, and in the lobby afterwards, I met a seventeen-year-old girl from Charlottetown, P.E.I., who had just started a girls' empowerment group called 24STRONG. She has a huge vision for where she wants to take her new initiative, and I am blown away by her ambition at her age.

Having that sense of purpose will act as a compass for her, which will help guide her decisions and her actions. And having that passion will help her continue to move forward toward her vision—toward her goal. Passion and purpose are the essential qualities to moving beyond the obstacles to achieving your goals—to still seeing the top of the mountain despite the dense fog that appears, or the top of the podium, despite the naysayers attempting to cloud your vision . . . even if you're able to see it only in your mind.

I wouldn't say that, growing up, I was unmotivated. But I was only pursuing goals that seemed like the next logical progression. Although I was still moving forward with my life, and, for all intents and purposes was successful at doing what I was doing, there wasn't any fuel behind the fire.

It took an immediate challenge—a very short-term goal with the highly unlikely desired outcome of competing in the Olympics less than five months after starting a new sport—for me to discover that I am motivated by challenges. The bigger the challenge, the more motivated I seem to be. If someone had told me that I could be an Olympic champion if I just trained really hard for four years, I never would have done it. In fact, someone *did* tell me that back during my undergraduate years when I was competing as a sprinter on the track team. I remember walking toward the door to leave after running indoor 300-metre and 4 x 400 metre relay races and being approached by a gentleman who, I believe, was officiating at the track meet. He told me that, based on what he had just seen, if I trained specifically for the event, I could most likely compete in the Olympics in the 400 metres. I *hated* running the 400-metre race. It was so painful and I found the lactic acid in my legs to be unbearable. I would sometimes even try to get out of running it because of the horrible feeling afterwards! I can't even remember how I responded to that man, but I'm sure I thanked him politely and, as quickly as the words left my mouth, dismissed the idea entirely from my mind. Apparently, the possibility of becoming an Olympian was not incentive enough to go through the training and the pain. The *why* of going to the Olympics was not a deep enough *why* for me to train for years for an unknown outcome.

But bobsledding was a different story. Not because I loved the sport (although I certainly learned to enjoy aspects of it), but I loved the challenge: the challenge of seeing if I could learn a new sport well enough and in time enough to qualify and compete in the Olympic Games that would be held only five months later. That *was* reason enough to set a short-term goal, which did involve the Olympics. But it took the catalyst of directly *experiencing* a testing camp to see the possibilities and to light the fire within me. My *root why* drove me to meet that very specific challenge. And in going for it, I pushed myself harder than I ever had before, showing myself that I was capable of *way more* than I had ever thought possible. See the power of discovering your *why*?

If you don't know what your fuel is, if you haven't found your passion, just keep moving forward. Commit to moving

It wasn't about winning—it was about what winning would enable. It wasn't about success— it was about purpose.

forward, learning new things, and experiencing new things. Increased exposure to new people and situations will increase your self-awareness of what you don't enjoy as well as what brings you the most happiness. So if you don't yet know what your *root why* is, set yourself the goal of trying new things. By continuing to move forward, you are increasing the likelihood of crossing paths with the catalyst that will fuel the fire inside you. And then? Brace yourself for a passion-filled, direction-filled, and purpose-driven life.

I realized at that testing camp in 2005 that I am motivated by challenges. And, as the years passed, I began to realize that the bigger the challenge, the more unachievable the desired outcome likely is, the more motivated I am. Perhaps to prove to others that it can be done. Perhaps to see how good I can be—to fulfill my potential and discover what I am truly capable of. Perhaps both. But I have also realized that a big challenge is not my biggest motivator—it is not my ultimate reason, my *root why*.

Self-Discovery

Sometimes it takes another person to show us something we wouldn't have seen before: a solution to a problem, a hidden opportunity, a different perspective. After a stressful 2008–09 World Cup bobsleigh season, I was on the verge of walking away from my goal to reach the Olympic podium in Vancouver and return to occupational therapy. It was my dad who shifted my perspective, which is all it took to keep me going. A shift. He simply made me think about my situation in a different way, which revealed my *root why*.

While attending a meeting in Toronto, he picked me up for dinner. I remember it vividly. We were in his rental car and I was frustrated and upset. I told him about everything that was going on with bobsledding, everything I was dealing with. It's not that they were issues uncommon in amateur sports, but they were new, and troubling, to me— the political manoeuvrings, tensions, and small-p power struggles. I told him how I didn't think trying to win a medal was worth the mental stress it all. It was more than I thought I had signed up for. More than I thought anyone should have to deal with.

Dad listened to everything I said and nodded, acknowledging that he could see how difficult and frustrating it must be. And then, in only the way a wise man can do (and anyone who's met my father would understand his ability to do this), without telling me what he thought I should do he simply commented that he never thought it was about winning a medal for me. That he had thought it was about the number of people I could impact. He just casually commented on the sheer number of people I could inspire simply by pursuing my Olympic podium goal, let alone potentially winning a medal on *home soil*. At the time, I think he and I were *both* thinking only of my family and friends, my community, maybe my Island... and had no idea the extent to which I could make a difference in so many people's lives. A *lot* of difference, as it turns out.

I never imagined that my success in sports would offer me the opportunity to influence so many people in a significant way. I loved the career of occupational therapy because it gave me the chance to inspire and motivate my clients, one-on-one, to see their challenging situations from a different perspective, to help them identify their priorities and goals, and then help break down those goals to facilitate achieving success and their desired outcomes. And now I do that for rooms full of people, speaking from the stage, or working with groups.

My dad's perspective made me realize that the goal of winning a medal at the Olympics wasn't enough to make me want to continue, but the thought of positively impacting people and making a difference in their lives *was* enough. It wasn't about winning—it was about what winning would enable. It wasn't about success—it was about purpose. Realizing that my motivation to compete at the Olympics was perfectly consistent with what motivated me as an occupational therapist was empowering; the only difference was that I'd be reaching people in a different way, and possibly be able to motivate them on a bigger scale, on a bigger stage, and in larger numbers.

Nothing had changed at my core, but seeing myself with a new perspective allowed me to apply myself and to adjust and stretch the limits of my goals to realize much more potential that I even knew I had. Knowing my *root why* gave me the motivation to keep going and to do what it took to eventually stand at the top of the Olympic podium. Twice. Even now I'm following the same motivation in my speaking career and with this book. And I might never have discovered that I was truly capable of it all had I not stepped back, shifted my perspective, and *come from away*—to see things in a different way, to discover my true purpose.

As I've mentioned, the introduction to bobsledding made me realize that I am motivated by challenges. But that conversation with my dad made me realize that I am much more deeply and powerfully motivated by inspiring and empowering others—my *root why*!

And so when I asked myself if joining the expedition to pursue the goal of summiting the highest mountain in Antarctica would be worth the struggle, would be worth the discomfort that would surely be involved, I was able to say, undoubtedly, *Yes*! It was easy to find the motivation to accept this monumental physical and mental challenge because the organization it was supporting and its goals aligned so perfectly with my purpose and my *root why*. So, climb the highest mountain in Antarctica? Challenge accepted!

A GLIMPSE OF ANOTHER PERSPECTIVE...

The people I met on that Antarctic expedition were some of the most selfless people I have ever met in my life, the civilians and soldiers alike, and their reasons for being there truly affected me, as did the experience. But the full impact hit me only after the experience was put into a different perspective for me by one soldier after our return to base camp. He pointed out that, as civilians, we had just experienced a sliver of what soldiers go through—a *glimpse* of what it's like to be deployed: removed from civilization and anything normal, isolated from loved ones, and dropped into a hostile environment with harsh and unfamiliar conditions in which, if you are not vigilant in looking out for yourself and for each other, something could very possibly kill you. Although in our case, it was more likely to be because of the freezing cold temperatures, an unexpected crevasse, or sliding down the side of a mountain instead of a bullet from combat or an IED. His perspective had a profound effect on me. I could never pretend to understand fully what it is like to put your life on the line for your country's freedom. But through that experience in Antarctica—the harsh conditions of the mountain, the very personal and emotional stories from the soldiers—and thanks to that one soldier's perspective, I do have a better appreciation for what the members of our Armed Forces endure. For us.

Don't Sell Yourself Short

Remember that the whole purpose of goal-setting, finding your *root why*, stepping outside of your comfort zone, and developing milestones and action plans is so that you can turn your dreams into reality. So you can discover your full potential and push yourself to see what you are capable of.

With his permission, I want to tell you the story of Sergeant Thomas White. While I was safely training to represent my country in the Vancouver Olympics (a goal many would consider ambitious), his eight-wheeled armoured reconnaissance vehicle—called the COYOTE—had hit an IED (improvised explosive device) in Afghanistan on March 20, 2009. His driver and the GIB (guy the back) were killed. And in February 2010, while I was waiting to run down an icy track, Thomas was having one of the seventeen surgeries he's had to have to save his life and mend his body.

In all, Thomas had three surgeries in Afghanistan before even being shipped home, where he then saw three more surgeons for fourteen more operations, six other doctors, three psychiatrists, and one psychologist. After one of his most recent operations, the nurses could not wake him for an hour as he was apparently deeply reliving the IED strike in his sleep. He went through intense physiotherapy to try to avoid more surgeries and, hopefully, to get his life back to some kind of 'normalcy'. But, in fact, the surgeries may not stop there because although he is working with a dental unit to rehabilitate his jaw, he may still need surgery for it at some point, as it keeps dislocating.

Thomas hoped that having the goal of reaching the summit of Mount Vinson in Antarctica (on the same expedition I went on with the True Patriot Love Foundation) would push him further along in his recovery. Of course, the *point* of the expedition was to raise awareness for PTSD, and having been through what he had experienced, he of all people profoundly knew the psychological impact of war. The healing process had been long, and he had made a lot of progress. But he wasn't yet in the shape he needed to be in to do the job he had been trained for in the military, and he had already been bypassed for promotion by some of his peers. He thought this climbing challenge would make a difference.

All of Thomas's doctors told him not to join the expedition—that he shouldn't attempt climbing a mountain in his condition, let alone climbing one in the most remote location on earth. But he chose to go anyway, and did so with Master Corporal Steven Rice, the gunner—and one of the two other survivors who had been in his tank when it was blown up.

And guess what? Thomas made it all the way to High Camp (3,773 metres/12,379 feet).

Because his back and hip had been giving him some trouble the day before, Thomas chose not to attempt the last climbing day, forfeiting the possibility of summiting the Vinson Massif. This decision was not based on self-limiting beliefs, however, but on facts and selflessness. Facts: He was already experiencing some pain, and the most gruelling day hadn't even started yet. Selflessness: If he *did* decide to attempt and wasn't able to make it the whole way (a nine- to twelve-hour return trip, covering 14 kilometres/8.75 miles return, 1,120 metres/3,670 feet of ascent with gradual 400 slopes and a rocky ridge on the summit pyramid, reaching the summit at 4,892 metres/16,050 feet), then his entire rope team—one guide and three other team members—would have to turn around and head back to High Camp with him. Thomas didn't want to take the possibility of summiting away from any of his teammates.

After hours and hours of trekking and climbing, the rope teams sporadically arrived back at High Camp from the summit, and Thomas was there to welcome everyone.

He was outwardly so happy and excited for everyone—for the whole team—but it wasn't hard to see the undercurrent of disappointment he felt because he hadn't summited. That had been his goal, after all: to reach the top. When I asked him how he felt, he said he felt like he had failed.

All Thomas needed was a different perspective on his success—a reminder of how far he'd come, what he had already accomplished, and the obstacles he'd had to deal with to do so. He would never have discovered that he was even capable of getting to High Camp of Mount Vinson had he not set his goal so high (both literally and figuratively).

As I mentioned, there are no guarantees when setting goals. Thomas may not have summited that day, but without him believing it was possible, he would never even have taken the first step of signing up for the expedition. He would never have discovered how far he could go and what he was capable of had he listened to those doctors and let *them* set his goals based on *their* perspective of what was possible. Thomas didn't care about so-called 'realistic' goals. He knew that 'realistic' goals are subjective, limiting self-fulfilling prophecies, that can only get you so far. I explained to him that, unlike many people, he had set his goals high enough to stretch himself and actually see what he was *really* capable of.

Thomas did not summit the mountain that day, and neither did five other climbers from our team who tried to make it but had to turn back. But it was not for lack of effort. And it was not because of assumptions, fears, self-limiting beliefs, or excuses. They went as far as they could on that particular day. They discovered what they were truly capable of...

on that particular day, on that particular expedition, at that particular point in their lives. Maybe their summit day is still to come.

Do your goals match your dreams? Are you setting your goals high enough?

I invite you to *embrace* discomfort and be fuelled and motivated by challenges, like Thomas White—and like me! Realize that it's not always going to feel good. But also realize that amazing things are possible. Don't sell yourself short— believe in the possibilities of what you are capable of. Don't put a limit on your potential or the potential of your family, friends, children, students, team, co-workers, business, company, organization, community...

In the end, if you fall short—and you will fall short sometimes if you set your goals high enough—don't let it be because it wasn't your best effort. See it as an isolated incident, and let your so-called *failure* be only a temporary indication of what your limits were at that moment. Failure to achieve a big goal will almost always still get you further than successfully achieving a small goal. But what *is* certain is that without reaching a point of failure, you will never discover the possibilities that lie within your abilities. So set your goals high, and when someone comments that they are big, lofty, or ambitious, just smile quietly and say, "I know."

And remember to celebrate how far you have come and what you did manage to accomplish! With growth, your limits change. So, when you *do* finally reach that high bar—your desired outcome—raise that bar a little higher, pick a higher mountain, and continue to climb.

11

PURSUE

Move Toward Your Goal

ONCE YOU HAVE established what you *really* want, have turned your dream into a goal by creating a plan of action for achieving it, have a clear vision of everything that is involved, know that it aligns with your values, and have made the conscious choice to take that step out of your comfort zone to *go for it*, it is time to put your plan into action. It is time to actively *pursue* that goal.

Plans tend to be made in an idealistic way—a straight line from Point A to Point B (or Point Z, depending on how many steps your plan has). But rarely does *anyone* reach a desired outcome without some kind of hiccup, detour, or need for re-evaluating (and sometimes recreating) the plan.

As we've already seen, obstacles may prevent some people from ever turning their dream into goals, and for those who have the courage to take that step, this pursuit phase can be a minefield. Very rarely do successful people reach their goals without having to overcome certain obstacles along the way.

Because of this, for some, this is the most challenging phase of achieving one's goals. It involves the most effort and skill development, and really tests one's commitment to the plan.

This is the phase in which 'shit happens', and the execution phase *truly* reveals what outcomes are *worth* struggling for.

The roadblocks you encounter can present themselves as minor events, like a delay in receiving necessary information in time to chair an important meeting. Or they can sometimes be life-altering, like an unexpected (and, perhaps, unwanted) pregnancy. Regardless of what the obstacle is, it can be perceived as being 'the end of the world', considered to be an insurmountable obstacle to achieving your goal, stopping you in your tracks; or simply an interruption—a minor hiccup in the big scheme of things—to executing the plan to accomplishing your goal. Keep in mind, external obstacles only become obstacles or roadblocks if your internal obstacles are given power. Being aware of what they are, combined with the *come from away* perspective, immediately helps take some of that power away.

In other words, how you view those unexpected events and situations in life will determine whether you see them as challenges and obstacles or unexpected opportunities to change course, to redirect your efforts toward a new and different goal (now referred to as 'pivoting' in business), or to get to your desired outcome by taking a different path. Something that initially appears to be an obstacle may give you pause enough to re-evaluate you plan, or even re-evaluate your priorities to see if your goal still ranks in the same place on the list. Have your priorities changed? Does this goal seem as important as it used to? Is there a better way to attain it? Do you feel as passionate about reaching or achieving the original goal as you once did? As we shall see, your attitude has a lot to do with whether or not you will achieve your goals and reach your full potential. Your frame of mind in the pursuit of your dreams can make the difference in getting there.

"Most of us spend too much time on what is urgent and not enough time on what is important."

STEPHEN R. COVEY

Focus on What Matters

Think about everything you try to squeeze into a day. How often do you wish there were more than twenty-four hours in the day to work with? Once you take away sleep hours, and time to eat, you're left cramming things into thirteen or fourteen hours of the day, and, in most cases, at least seven hours are spent at work or school from Monday to Friday. That leaves only six or seven hours a day for everything else. That's all anyone gets. When you have a goal, it's important to make the best of the time you have available to work toward it.

In fact, I believe that there *are* enough hours in the day. And everyone has the same number. It all comes down to being able to focus on your priorities and manage distractions. Think about it: I have *only* six or seven hours a day to do what I want and need to do? Now shift perspective: Wow! I *get* six or seven hours a day to focus on what's important to me? Even if a couple of hours per day needs to go toward a commute, for example, you still end up with four or five hours a day for you. That's twenty to twenty-five hours just from Monday to Friday. And that's a whole extra twenty-four-hour day! Now, what could you do with an extra day a week? Could you carve out even more time to focus on your priorities? If you watched just one hour less of TV a day, that's seven more hours—one whole workday!

The problem is that distractions are everywhere: texts, emails, social media notifications, pop-ups, the very comfy couch in the corner, and a wandering mind. But, again, you have a choice: use distractions as an excuse or learn how to manage those distractions and reach your goal despite them.

We all want to use our time more effectively, but even as I wrote the first part of this section, I was interrupted by two phone calls that *I* made, that were initiated by a notification that popped up on my computer screen, reminding me of something that I needed to take care of before the end of the day. After I made my calls, I also thought a quick glance at Twitter wouldn't hurt, and noticed three text messages that I thought I would *quickly* respond to. I admit it: I have a problem of being distracted. Ha! Admitting it is the first step.

I quickly realized, however, that I needed to regain my focus. So I turned off the Wi-Fi on my computer, put my phone on silent, and changed my writing screen to the "focus" screen, a plain black screen with no clock or editing buttons to visually distract me. I also set an alarm to go off after an hour and a half of working, seeing as ninety minutes is, generally, the maximum amount of time that people can focus before needing a break. After an hour of focused effort, I was already more productive that I had been the hour before.

Maximizing your time is not only important to feeling productive but to actually *being* productive, enabling you to do all the things you need to do, as well as all the things you *want* to do, moving you closer and closer to achieving your goals and the life you want. But many of us find it hard to carve out the time necessary to pursue our big dreams when there don't seem to be enough hours in the day to do all the things that *need* to be done. But maybe that's just a matter of perspective too.

I recently listened to a great TED Talks podcast by Laura Vanderkam about how to gain control of your free time. Free time? you say. What's *that*? Well, you may be able to create more of it than you think. Vanderkam conducted a study of extremely busy women, having them write time diaries about their work and sleep habits, and anything else they were doing with their time. One extremely busy woman came home one evening to find that her water heater had broken, and there was water all over her basement. She had to deal with the immediate aftermath that evening, plumbers the next day, and a professional cleaning crew the day after that. Based on her time diary, she spent a total of seven hours in her week dealing with this unexpected event. Vanderkam pointed out that if she had been asked at the start of the week if she could find seven hours in the week to train for a triathlon, or seven hours to mentor some worthy people, the response would most likely have been "Can't you see how busy I am?" Vanderkam suggested that the key to time management is treating our priorities as the equivalent of that broken water heater, marking them as 'urgent' or 'important' in our calendars, and that how you spend every minute is your *choice*.

Practise Intentionality

Knowing what your goal is puts purpose behind your actions. It means you are doing what you are doing for a specific reason. You are not going to achieve your goal by accident. You must take steps that will move you closer to where you want to end up. This is called *intentionality*. Being intentional with your choices, your scheduling, and even your thoughts will make a huge difference in the quality of your growth, as well as the speed in which you experience that progress.

As I mentioned, I wasn't a very driven person when I was younger. It wasn't that I didn't care. It was that I wasn't focused. I didn't have a goal, so I had no reason to be intentional in my choices or my actions.

But when I suddenly took on the goal of seeing if I could qualify for the Canadian National Bobsleigh Team and compete in the Torino Olympics in less than five months, I suddenly became *very* intentional. When I was back in Toronto, even climbing stairs became very intentional. Not simply to get to the top but as an opportunity to develop my pushing abilities. That may sound a bit odd to you, but I assure you that as I would climb the stairs two at a time, I would make sure to extend my push-off leg on the stair and fully squeeze/contract my glute (my bum—a big power muscle). Instead of wasting that time, I intentionally made climbing stairs an opportunity for growth. Intentionality is important in making large decisions or taking large actions, but it can be just as important and effective when dealing with smaller actions. Climbing the stairs to get to the top is one thing. But climbing the stairs as a way to get to the top of the *podium* is a whole different story, and it all comes down to intent.

HOW MANY TIMES have you *decided* to do something? That *this* was going to be the year to lose that baby weight you've been carrying around for the past two years? That *this* was going to be the year to get certified in the next level of qualifications for your job to move up the ladder? How many times have you *decided* to do something but didn't act? You need to be intentional in making a plan in the first place, but you also have to be intentional with your actions along the way.

Almost a year ago, my mother and her friend asked me if I would go to the gym with them and show them some exercises. A few were exercises they had been shown before, but they hadn't been told to think of them intentionally. I told them they needed not to just go through the motions of an exercise but to think of the *point* of the exercise. Which muscles (or, at least, which area) were they targeting with the exercise? And then the point became about feeling *it*—the workout—in that particular area, and if they didn't feel it where they were supposed to, then they were compensating with a different part of their body. Intentionality promotes efficiency and effectiveness, not just with the approach to overall goals but with the execution of individual steps and actions.

Are you being intentional with your choices, or are you letting someone else choose your path? Are you actually making conscious choices about your career, about how your life will be, or are you just floating along in the same old, same old routine because it simply seems good enough?

Create a Supportive Environment

Obstacles are inevitable on your path to living up to your full potential, so it's important to prepare yourself mentally and emotionally for them—and even for outright failure if the risk you've taken doesn't pan out. As we've seen, achieving your dreams and stretch goals is often possible with the right attitude, the right mindset. One of the keys to all this is having a safe environment in which to take risks, whether you eventually succeed or fail. Ideally, your emotional safety-net starts with your parents and other influential adults in your life, but you can learn to develop a positive support network for yourself even if you didn't grow up in a supportive environment. Ensuring that you have safe environments, an emotional safety-net you can rely on, will enable you to take the risks involved in following your dreams, in putting yourself out there in pursuit of being the best you can be.

People often ask me how I developed such a level-headed view of winning and losing. My parents believed in providing my siblings and me with opportunities not only to do what we were good at but also to discover what we loved to do. They would sign us up for activities we expressed interest in, with the understanding that 1) money doesn't grow on trees, so once it's paid for, it's a commitment, and 2) that once committed to a team or group of any kind (whether there was a fee or not), that commitment would last until the end (defined as the end of a season or term, until there was a new registration or set of tryouts). At that point, we could re-evaluate whether we were still enjoying what we'd signed up for and if we wanted to continue with that particular activity and group.

The emphasis was never on winning when I grew up. It was all about effort. If we lost and were upset about the results, my parents simply asked if there was anything more we could have done, if we had done everything *we* could to contribute to the final result. And then we would go to Dairy Queen.

The true benefit of those Dairy Queen outings is that my siblings and I grew up knowing that the love and support of my parents was not contingent on winning. We didn't get an ice cream only if we won. We were celebrating good effort.

This is actually a very important concept, not only for parents but for CEOs and managers—in any environment in which progress is the goal. This support for effort regardless of the outcome creates a safe environment for taking risk—an environment in which people can *try* to see what they are capable of, be creative and innovative with their ideas, without the fear of being rejected, ridiculed, or judged ... or even fired for taking a misstep. These days, companies with the biggest growth are companies who give autonomy to their employees. An Australian software company gave their employees twenty-four hours of freedom to work on whatever they wanted to advance the company. They were not under supervision, were able to work on projects related to any department, and then presented their suggestions—whether brand-new ideas or solutions to issues—to the whole group. Often, the findings were so great that they were implemented by the company. This creative, supportive approach helped the company evolve and at the same time kept employees engaged in the overall running and success of the company.

My parents always gave me a safe place to explore my abilities. Meaning, they gave me a safe place to fail. This is where I developed a healthy attitude toward taking risks. My parents always made sure that if I did my best there was nothing else that needed to be done. No reason to be disappointed.

I AM EXTREMELY fortunate and grateful for the support of my family. I feel very lucky that they have always wanted to attend as many of my sporting events as they possibly can, whether it was in grade school or on the international stage. But as I started competing at higher levels, logistics became a bigger issue. Even as an adult, I wasn't immune to the thoughts of not wanting my parents to waste—or think they had wasted—time or money. My family, for example, had to decide in October 2005, when I first competed in the sport of bobsleigh, if they were going to go to the 2006 Torino Olympics four months later, even before I had qualified for the Olympic team. Time was of the essence to deal with the logistics: they had to arrange flights, hotels, and tickets *just in case* I ended up competing in the Games, when I had only ever competed in one race! And even if I *did* end up qualifying, there was no guarantee that I would be the brakeman racing. And even if I *did* end up competing in the Olympics, they would have travelled so far to watch me for mere *seconds* on the track!

The same scenario arose with rugby. Although the flights, hotel, and tickets didn't have to be secured as far in advance for the 2006 Rugby World Cup, and my family could wait until they knew that I had made the World Cup team, they were still committing to an unknown scenario—there were no guarantees that I would actually step on the field and play even a minute of one game in the tournament.

When I voiced my concern to my parents, *wanting* them to be there and appreciating the fact that *they* wanted to be there as well, but not knowing whether I would even be competing, and not wanting them to waste their time and money (or *think* that they had), my mother very calmly replied, "Heather, you should know this by now. We're not going to *watch* you. We're going to *support* you."

And that is sometimes why I feel like I had an advantage over others—you can never underestimate the power of unconditional love or support, regardless of where it comes from.

HAVING A SUPPORTIVE environment that makes room for failure is much more important than having an environment that only supports and acknowledges success. Whether I would win or lose at the Olympics meant nothing to my parents, except for the empathy for *my* feelings. When I won, they were happy *for* me because I had achieved something that I had wanted, and were proud *of* me because of the person I was and the *way* in which I achieved my goal. The only way I could've disappointed my parents would have been if I had become entitled and arrogant in the process or in the aftermath, which, unfortunately, happens to some people when they reach a certain level of success and recognition. My parents would have been disappointed in me if I had started treating other people as less important than I—not for losing.

Look for Opportunities and Solutions

When I lived in Trinidad, I dated a guy there for about eight months—which was, in hindsight, *probably* seven months too long. I finally ended it, as we just weren't very well matched. A few weeks later, I was walking back to my apartment while talking with my mother on the phone when I found a box at my door. On the outside of the box was a belated birthday card from the ex-boyfriend. Inside was . . .

"Oh. My. God. Ohmygod. Ohmygod. Ohmygod."

I repeated the words over and over as my mom begged me to tell her what was inside the box.

"Mom, it's a duck."

"You mean like a stuffed animal?"

"No, Mom! I mean a bright yellow fluffy *live* duckling!"

Silence. And then a burst of laughter at the other end of the phone.

A duck! What was I going to do with a duck? I called my ex-boyfriend. He said he knew Mom and I had a thing for ducks. Which was true. But it was an inside joke between the two of us. It started with a card Mom sent to me while I was at university about having my ducks in a row. Mom would wrap my birthday present in wrapping paper that had ducks on it. If either of us sees a funny duck card, we will send it to the other for any occasion. Duck cartoons found in newspapers or magazines get cut out and sent. Mom bought me duck pyjama bottoms once . . .

None of these involved, nor prepared me for, a *real duck*. I told my ex-boyfriend all this. I reminded him that I lived in an upstairs apartment, that the woman downstairs had two dogs that took over the yard during the days, and that I had to go back to Canada in less than four months.

"Okay," he said, "I can come pick up the duck tomorrow."
Good.

I hung up the phone closed the box and walked away. The duck then started squeaking. Ducks don't quack when they are little. They squeak. And it kept squeaking.

Squeak, squeak, squeak, squeak, squeak, squeak, squeak.

I finally opened the box and the squeaking stopped. Great, I figured I would just leave the box open and all would be quiet. I walked away. The squeaking started again. I walked back and peeked in. The squeaking stopped. So, I sat beside it with the box open for the rest of the evening.

By the time I wanted to go to sleep, my duckling companion didn't, and it just kept squeaking. Maybe it wanted to get out of the box? I scooped it up and put it on the bathroom floor (which was tiled and any messes could be easily cleaned up). It stopped squeaking... until I closed the door. And not only did it start squeaking again but also started running back and forth, with its beak poking out from underneath the door. I opened the door carefully, thinking it was going to run into the apartment, but it didn't go anywhere. It just quietly looked up at me.

I wrapped a pillow with a towel and put it on the bathroom floor and laid down on the floor on my stomach with my arms up on the pillow and my hands tucked under one of my cheeks. Good night! I closed my eyes. That was when I felt the pillow move. I opened my eyes to see the little duckling crawl up over my arm, curl up and bury its beak in the crook of my arm, and... close its eyes.

You have got to be kidding me. What was I going to do now?

The next day, my ex-boyfriend showed up to take the duck back.

"What's going to happen to it?" I asked him.

"It's going to go back to the farm, grow, and then someone will most likely eat it."

How could I give it back, knowing that it would be eaten? But how could I keep it? I didn't *want* to own a duck. The duck squeaked.

But this one? How could I let him take it? I didn't want it to be eaten. I sent my ex away empty-handed. Jump first, think later?

I proceeded to name the duck Rugger and kept him until I left Trinidad three-and-a-half months later. Just like bob-sledding, Rugger was a gift I never knew I wanted. He went from being an impossible pet in my mind to something that made me *want* to think of solutions. How many times do we say, "We can't" or "It's an impossible situation" without actually giving it much thought, letting our fears, assumptions, and self-limiting beliefs get in the way, when all it would really take is a different perspective and some manoeu-vring, reorganizing, or reprioritizing? Maybe some creative thinking?

The more we genuinely open ourselves up to the idea of possibilities and opportunities, the more we think about how to bridge the gap with solutions, not excuses. A positive mindset begets positive actions.

It's interesting how, when you really want something, you figure out a way to make it work. Or when something comes up that you don't necessarily want but *need* to deal with. How many times do we say that we just don't have *time* to do some-thing? But then, when an unexpected emergency comes up, we are able to find or rearrange time to accommodate it (like that broken water pipe I discussed earlier).

But when you *don't* want something (or don't want it *badly* enough to struggle for it), all you see are obstacles, and think about the ways that it *won't* work—that it could *never* happen. Excuses are suddenly on the tip of your tongue.

That duck shifted my perspective. And I suddenly saw all the ways I could keep it.

And I did keep it until I needed to return home. I was heartbroken to have to leave Rugger behind. I wanted to bring him back to Canada, but quarantine rules prevented that—Rugger would surely have gone missing and would have become someone's dinner while he waited the standard three months to clear customs in Trinidad, where duck curry is a much-loved meal. Some guys on the rugby team used to tease me by calling Rugger 'Peking' and, when it was time for me to leave, joked about the idea of me donating Rugger to the club— that he would be a good meal for the team! (I'm pretty sure they were only *half* joking! Ugh!) But I had to do *something* with him. So I left him with a vegetarian family.

THE STORY OF Rugger and my delayed willingness to open up to that experience (which turned out to be a surprisingly great one) may seem like a bit of a stretch in relation to achieving one's potential, but it's not. It's actually quite a good metaphor for being open to ideas and experiences because, without exposure and experience, you will never know what joy you may be denying yourself. You may never discover a new passion, a new path, a new area of potential that can be tapped. Another area in which you may excel.

Had I not eventually been open to owning a duck, I would not have experienced the joy he gave me every time I returned home from work, running to the door to greet me, while squawking and, literally, *wagging* his tail. I may not have realized that simply making the mental shift to believing in the possibilities inherent in *anything* is itself a catalyst to finding solutions within *any* situation, instead of dwelling on excuses. Had I not been open to the idea of flying down icy bobsleigh tracks at crazy speeds, I would have stayed on the path I had been on and would currently be working somewhere as an occupational therapist.

What goal are you pursuing now? And why are you pursuing it? Are you pursuing it with blinders on? Are you missing out on opportunities and possibilities because you are only focused on that one goal? And focused on achieving it in one particular way? Have you already turned down opportunities without giving them much thought because they didn't fit with your preconceived notion of what your life *should* be like? Or fit with your predetermined vision of how your life *will* turn out (even though it is based on our self-imposed limitations)? I want you to pursue your goals with passion and perseverance but *not* with blinders on—not at the expense of missing out on opportunities that may be more aligned with your path to personal excellence.

You are not stuck on one path... unless you *choose* to be.

I wasn't open to the idea of bobsleighing when Dennis first tried to recruit me to the sport in 2001, but had I not been open to the opportunity when it presented itself again in 2005, my life would not be what it is today. I didn't realize it at the time, but the choice of putting my master's degree on hold for one year to *try* a new sport as a challenge changed the course of my life.

Reporters used to ask me where I saw myself in five years. My only answer was that, if I knew exactly where I'd be in five years, I'd be disappointed in myself because that would mean pursuing a goal with blinders on—not being open to potential opportunities that might present themselves along the way. That may sound counter-intuitive, considering that this is a section about pursuing one's goals, but you must understand that sometimes we don't know what we want until the opportunity shows up. Remember, the dreams that we actually choose to turn into goals are limited by our awareness and our experiences.

I do not mean that you should be distracted by every opportunity that comes along. But every time a new opportunity presents itself, it is simply a chance to evaluate all the possibilities that exist within that potential path, reassess your priorities, and *choose* the direction you want to take. Purposefully and intentionally. *Choose* which path you want to take. *Choose* which goal you want to pursue from that point on. Because you are not stuck on one path . . . unless you *choose* to be.

Find Opportunities in Setbacks

Sometimes, even obstacles and distractions can present themselves as opportunities, if you look at them the right way. Don't focus on the disruption to your original plan and the barrier to achieving your original goal. Instead, remain open to opportunities and the possibilities, no matter what the situation. Now, most distractions and obstacles are just that—and you don't want to go there—but if you assess them carefully against your circumstances, goals, and values, you may just find this disruption is a different kind of catalyst prompting you to change course, charting a new path to your potential with its *own* goals and challenges.

After the Vancouver Olympics in February 2010, the other bobsledders took two months off, as they normally would at the end of a season. I took two weeks and then started training for the Rugby World Cup at the end of the summer. In that September tournament, fifteen minutes into our final game, I destroyed my right ankle. I had already committed to competing in the upcoming bobsleigh season that winter. So, I rehabbed that entire fall and was able to go back and compete in three races and the World Championships in early 2011.

But I knew during those few races that my ankle was not entirely healed. When I did any kind of high-impact work, it would swell up and be sore for two days. As a result, I could train only one day on the track (two runs to figure out timing and distance for loading into the sled at that particular track) and then race a few days later when the swelling had gone down. That was it. The rest of the time I iced and elevated my leg. No extra training or lifting. Following the World Championships, where Kaillie and I claimed bronze, I realized that if I wanted to compete seriously in anything again, I was going to have to do more to rehab my ankle completely.

I saw a sports doctor in Toronto who was astounded that I had been able to compete at all, considering the injury to my ankle. I had crushed my cartilage, had micro-fractures throughout four of the bones in my ankle, and completely ruptured my anterior talofibular ligament (ATFL)—the ligament at the front of my ankle. It was not an easy injury to heal while still being active. So, for rehab, he suggested I do track cycling. At first I thought he was crazy, as he was very well aware that I am a sprinter and *not* an endurance athlete, but he explained that track cycling involves sprinting around a track. I could keep up my strength and power output without putting any impact on my ankle, and maybe I would enjoy it.

So, I bought a road bike. Not having ever ridden a 'skinny-wheeled' bike before, I figured the first step would be to learn how to clip in and out of pedals. Nothing like starting right at the basics. It was June 2011.

In August, I watched a track cycling competition live for the first time and met up with the national coach, who put me through some power testing on my road bike. Based on those results, I was invited to train in Los Angeles with the Canadian team for the winter. This unplanned therapy was beginning to have possibilities.

At the end of January 2012, I was told that at the end of that February, I would be given a time trial. And if I beat the standard for the 500-metre sprint, I could join the national team to compete in the Pan American Track Cycling Championships in Argentina in March (only a week after my tryout). I had my audition, and within days I was on that flight to Argentina with the team, where I placed fourth in that event. Never planned for that to happen!

The team then asked me to do the match sprint time trial, which I had *never done before*! My first reaction was to say *no* (which I did). I was freaked out with the closeness of other wheels to mine, and it was a race based on strategy, which comes with experience, which I did not have. But the team needed another sprinter to help get more points to secure a qualifying spot for the London Olympics that summer. This was all about my teammate. If I could help earn points for the team, it would secure her qualifying spot on the Olympic team. Even if I placed *last,* I would earn the team some points.

I ended up finishing fifth! That result actually made *me* eligible for the Olympics in London that summer. But there is a difference between being eligible and qualifying. Had our team had enough points (which are accumulated over two years) to qualify *two* spots at the Olympics, I might actually have found myself there!

Competing in the Pan American Track Cycling Championships in Argentina made track cycling the third sport in which I have been honoured to wear the maple leaf on my chest and represent my country. I would never have seen that opportunity as a possibility had I not injured my ankle so badly in that rugby game.

I have learned over the years that setbacks (obstacles to achieving our goals) are often one of two things: 1) a forced pause on our current journey; a chance to look around and take in the scenery, to re-evaluate if our current destination is still our *desired* outcome, whether the path we are on is still in alignment with our values and priorities, or whether we see a better opportunity that we would have missed had we continued along that path as we were; or 2) a straight-up test to see how badly we want that thing we are dreaming of.

Tap into Your Grit

Award-winning psychologist Angela Duckworth took the world by storm when, in 2016, she published her book *Grit: The Power of Passion and Perseverance*. Based on her research and her own personal experiences, she concluded that *grit*—'a passionate persistence'—is the secret to outstanding achievement. According to Duckworth, identifying our passions and following through on our commitments, regardless of external factors, is more crucial to success than natural talent.

I would add that first *believing* in the possibilities and in your ability to achieve them is essential to reaching one's goals. But belief is not enough. I have to agree with her that grit is a critical element in achieving our potential because passion is what makes it all worth pursuing despite the obstacles, and the perseverance helps us get beyond the setbacks. Grit *is* essential to executing your goals. Because trying to discover what you are capable of is not always smooth sailing. In fact, pushing yourself to your full potential is *not* smooth sailing at all.

What I didn't mention earlier about my short-track cycling stint, and what the media usually isn't privy to, is what was going on behind the scenes—what it took for me to even get that tryout to join the national team at the Pan American Track Cycling Championships. Because sometimes, although *you* may believe in the possibilities, the assumptions, fears, or limiting beliefs of *others* can be more of an external obstacle standing in the way of your goals.

After I put up some impressive numbers when I was initially tested in Montreal with the power metre on my road bike, the team's excitement about my explosive power was growing, especially as I had never been on a track before. They got me out there to Los Angeles and, after only a week and a half, wanted to test my speed and power, and...

I crashed. I split the fascia and tore the muscle in my thigh.

I went back to Ontario to rehab for the month of October, but when I returned it seemed as though the cyclist who originally thought I would have made a good team sprint partner didn't believe that I would recover well enough (or in time) to compete that year. Seeing as it was less than a year out from the London Olympics, she decided to focus all her energy in training for the individual events that she would hopefully qualify for. My goal was not to compete on the bike in the Olympics that summer, but I went back to Los Angeles anyway. Even if she didn't think I would be ready to be her teammate for the team sprint, my goal was to be able to represent my country, to earn a spot to compete for Canada in *any* race. So, I decided to focus on my own development—on representing myself.

The coaches, however, had also moved on. They told me that I could no longer train with the team because they were focusing on the athletes who were going to the 2012 Summer Olympics. I asked if I could still train for a World Cup race and again was told that they were focusing only on the athletes who were going to the Olympics.

Yeah, I was super annoyed and frustrated as I headed home for Christmas. I stopped training. I thought, *What's the point?* Then, I remembered I wasn't training for *them*; I was training for me. I would find a way to pursue my goal, and only stop training when *I* was ready to ... with no regrets.

I went back to Los Angeles mid-January and started training again on my own. I was there for a week when I ran into the coach at an indoor competition. She told me she had spoken to the other coaches and felt they should have given me at least the opportunity to compete

Okay! Great!

Then they told me the Home Depot velodrome we had been training on was going to be closed for two weeks during that month for another competition. So I went out and found another club. I trained with a group of guys who basically adopted and challenged me. Goals have a way of making you find a way when confronted with things standing in your way. Sometimes you just have to power through the obstacles to get to where you want to go.

Life presents us with obstacles, whether they are injuries or financial restrictions, or something totally different, and forces us into deciding what we are going to do with them. We are faced with a choice: Are we going to accept them as a challenge and persevere with grit? Or are we going to passively let them dictate the story of our lives?

My injuries have been challenges that I have chosen to persevere through. While the decision to do that was easy sometimes, it wasn't in some cases. Evaluating whether the pursuit is *worth* the struggle is natural and, if it is, then put all your grit to the test to push through to discover your *way more*.

INJURIES?... YES. REGRETS?... NO.

March 1996: Right ankle sprain and fracture (basketball)

December 2001: Fractured radius bone, wrist (rugby)

December 2003: Fractured spine (rugby)

March 2006: Back of head split open (rugby, but not on the field of play—fainted in a hotel)

May 2008: Avulsion fracture, right shoulder (rugby)

January 2009: Friction burn on bum and lost feeling on fingertips (bobsleigh)

July 2009: Stress reaction (early stages of stress fracture), right shin (bobsleigh)

September 2010: Destroyed right ankle—cartilage crushed, micro-fractures in four anklebones, completely ruptured ATFL (rugby)

September 2011: Split fascia and tore muscle, left thigh (cycling)

November 2012: Surgery, right hip (believed to be overuse injury after years of training for so many sports)

November 2014: Surgery, left hip (believed to be overuse injury after years of training for so many sports)

This is my list of just the major injuries I sustained while playing sports, most of which you've heard about in this book. It doesn't include minor sprains or strains, charley horses or scratches, bruises or black eyes. But none of them make me regret my choices to compete, and I have no regrets about anything I did to make myself better and get back into competition.

Identify the Silver Lining

Yes, there will be roadblocks you'll have to face in the journey to achieving your goals. But whether you are ultimately able to live to your full potential depends entirely on your attitude to the obstacles in your way. Are they truly roadblocks preventing you from getting to where you want to go? Or are they simply detours, taking you on a different route that may impart more wisdom along the way? Or are they diverting you to another path entirely, and to accomplishing a different and equally (or more) fulfilling goal?

People who tend to give up in the face of challenges to their plans tend to be less successful in life, to settle for the path of least resistance, not standing up to the challenges but giving in to them. People who are successful in life, however, face those roadblocks head-on and try to find a way around them to get to where they want to be. Studies showed that it takes only sixty seconds after hearing about a problem for a successful person to start coming up with solutions.

MICHAEL TAIT, ONE of the civilians on the Antarctica expedition with me in January 2016, told me he had heard that high-performance athletes work in a similar way: they tend to put a positive spin on an otherwise negative situation. When I asked him what he meant, he recalled a story about our trip to Antarctica, which had happened only a month or two earlier. It was something very simple, but it had stuck with him.

Our whole expedition group flew to Antarctica by way of Santiago, Chile, and then to Punta Arenas, Chile (on the south coast), where we stayed for two days before flying on a large Russian cargo plane to Union Glacier, Antarctica. We had to switch airlines in Santiago, which meant collecting our luggage and putting it through security before checking it in again. The woman organizing the logistics of the whole thing was amazing, managing a group of almost thirty people, and we were all quickly shuffled through doors on the way to our next gate. As we were walking, I noticed Michael standing off to the side, dialing something into his phone, and I asked him if everything was okay. He said out of *all* the luggage (two or three pieces per person), one of *his* bags was missing. As he recalled it, I didn't miss a beat, jokingly commenting on his genius planning. That he had clearly planned it so he wouldn't have to lug all of his heavy bags from the airport in Punta Arenas to the hotel . . . that he just *knew* it would roll up to the hotel in some conveyance, possibly on the back of a donkey (my ignorance of the area and where we were going clearly apparent in my comments). I was simply trying to make him laugh, but also to put things in perspective—that it was *not* the end of the world. But *he* was thinking about how that person had been right: successful athletes *do* tend to see the positive.

DURING THE TWO weeks (or so) we had off for the Christmas holidays during our 2009–10 bobsleigh World Cup season, I went back home to Prince Edward Island to visit my parents. My trainer, Matt Nichol, told me to take a whole week off and do nothing. Normally, I would have loved that directive, but with the Vancouver Olympics less than two months away, taking time off certainly didn't feel natural for me. But I trusted him. He said that we would "blast my system" after giving my body (including the nervous system) a rest. So I waited patiently for my program.

When I went back to the gym, I felt good, and I could understand what he was trying to do. But, seeing as I was in P.E.I. and he was in Toronto, I followed his programs while listening to feedback from my body, and then he and I would chat on the phone if I had any questions.

Well, one of the days had a split squat exercise in the rack, and it said to build up, adding a bit of weight with each set. But I found the first prescribed weight already heavy enough. I mean, it was *heavy*, and I didn't want to *injure* myself. But I also wasn't going to *not* do my workout. So I did all the sets I needed to, staying at the lowest suggested weight.

That night I called Matt. I was concerned that I couldn't add any weight to the bar when doing the exercise. Was I weaker than he expected me to be? Was I weaker than I should be at this point before the Olympics? Should I really have taken a *whole* week off?

Matt just listened quietly. And then, after a pause on the line, asked me one question: "Heather, tell me something. Were you lifting in kilos or pounds?"

Oh my gosh! The numbers he had put in my program were all in pounds, but I had been lifting in kilos! It didn't even occur to me. I had been lifting more than twice the weight Matt had indicated for me. I couldn't believe the mistake I had made.

Any athlete knows that if you put in a really good workout, you're going to feel it in your muscles the next day, but you will *really* feel it in your muscle the day *after* that—two days after the workout. And you know you're in trouble when you start feeling it later the same day of the workout.

Well, I was already feeling it in my glutes and my groin that evening (and by 'feeling it', I mean I was really sore), and while I spoke with Matt on the phone and realized my mistake, not only did I feel like an idiot, but I started to worry that I may have screwed up the training that I was supposed to do over the next few days—that my legs would be too sore to have effective training sessions.

Matt said, "Well, having lifted what you did, the bad news is that you're going to be really sore for the next few days. The *good* news is that we know you're really strong!"

Wow! Now *that's* perspective!

(I swear I could hear him smiling, eyes gleaming, on the other end of the phone.)

Check Your Mindset

It's much easier to cultivate and maintain a positive outlook if you have people like Matt rooting for you in your corner and encouraging you along the way. I think we can assume that praise and kind words are helpful to us no matter what, but it turns out that the type of praise and encouragement you get from others can affect how you behave. There are, in fact, different kinds of praise and, surprisingly to most people, it makes a difference. A testament to the power and impact of words.

Dr. Carol Dweck, professor of psychology at Stanford University, is one of the world's leading researchers on the topic of achievement, success, mindset, and motivation. I read her book *Mindset: The New Psychology of Success* a number of years ago, and I remember thinking that she had nailed the key to achievement. Dweck conducted a study of students going into seventh grade, at which point the work usually gets harder, grading gets more stringent, and the environment becomes less personal—a time when many kids start disliking school. She assessed their mindset before-hand—whether they had a fixed or growth mindset (whether they believed intelligence was fixed or could be developed).

The students had all started grade seven with almost iden-tical achievement test scores, but by the end of the first term, their grades had split apart based on which mindset they had, and they continued to diverge over the next two years. But why? Why did mindset have such a drastic effect on the outcomes of these students? Because they had different beliefs. Those with a *fixed* mindset believed that if you have ability, you shouldn't need effort. And if you need a lot of effort to accomplish something, it shows that you don't have a lot of ability. (Dweck believes this to be one of the worst beliefs one can have, and the reason why so many promising students don't fulfill their potential, simply coasting along. When they finally have to try—for example, suddenly arriving at university where much more is expected of them—they actually *can't* do it because they don't know *how* to put in effort, and they watch while others pass them by.) However, those students with a *growth* mindset believed that effort is what activates their abilities.

The students with a *fixed* mindset also believed that a setback or a deficiency in performance reveals their limitations and, therefore, they hide or run from their mistakes, or they try to conceal their deficiencies. Because of this, they have no way to handle difficulties. They become discouraged, want to give up, run away, become defensive (or act bored), or act out, blaming other people or things for their lack of effort or performance. The students with a *growth* mindset, however, believed that mistakes or setbacks are a natural part of learning—a natural occurrence when you take on challenges.

What a difference! Do any of those behaviours sound familiar to you? Do you recognize any of them in yourself?

But how are these mindsets developed? How is it that some people grow up believing that traits are permanent, and others grow up believing that people are evolving beings? Praise. Dweck has discovered through research that *praise* is the culprit. Or the catalyst. Specifically, praising children's

There is a
big difference
between
expecting to
succeed and
knowing you
are *capable* of
succeeding.

intelligence or abilities actually *harms* them by putting them in a *fixed* mindset. It turns them off to learning through challenges.

Dweck conducted another study to look at this. They had two groups of early adolescent teenagers, each given the same ten fairly difficult problems from a non-verbal IQ test. They all did well, and the examiners gave them all praise. However, each group received a different kind of praise:

1   Ability Praise: "Wow, you got [say] eight right. That's a really good score! You must be really *smart* at this."

2   Effort Praise (strategy, focus, persistence): "Wow, you got [say] eight right. That's a really good score. You must have *worked* really hard."

Immediately after receiving praise, the groups began to differ. When asked if they wanted a challenging task they could learn from, the kids who were praised for ability rejected the chance to learn in favour of something they were sure to do well on. They had already developed a fixed mindset and didn't want their natural 'ability' brought into question. Those who were praised for the effort overwhelmingly wanted the challenging task they could learn from. They didn't feel they were in jeopardy if they struggled for a while.

When later presented with even harder problems to solve, which the students didn't do so well on, the kids praised for ability lost their confidence and didn't enjoy the problems anymore. Their performance suffered even after going back to solving the easier problems. The kids who were praised for effort remained confident. They saw that the problems were more difficult but said they preferred the harder ones. *Their* performance flourished when asked to solve the easier problems again.

So, as you can see, the *kind* of praise you give to yourself and others can either help or hinder in the long run. You'll notice that I wrote *yourself*—as what we say to ourselves (that little voice in our heads) can be, and often is more, helpful or harmful to our progress and the possibility of fulfilling our potential. So be mindful of using the power and impact of words to inspire and motivate yourself, and others, to achieve *way more*.

Exercise Your Mental Toughness

It is a popular belief that elite athletes succeed because of their physical talents and their dedication to training. However, although that is often how they made it to that top level of competition, the athletes who succeed *within* that top level of competition do so because of their ability to deal with the psychological pressures of their sport. It is about being mentally tough enough to compete. And if you think I'm only referring to athletes, you are mistaken.

It has been said that winning (or success) is 90 percent mental and 10 percent physical. I don't believe that is the case *unless* referring to the highest level of performance. Below that level, the physical differences and technical skill level make too much of an impact, and this can be something as simple as physical size differences during puberty, to differences in skill development like throwing a football, or being able to speak well in front of a large group of people or just one.

But when you reach the highest level of competition—the highest level of performance in any industry—those physical differences in abilities no longer stand out. It has, generally, become a level playing field, with only 10 percent of variance in the physical skills required to execute the job. When you get to the level where everyone's skillsets are generally the same—elite—it is the mental game that will make the difference, that will determine who has the champion mindset. And, at that point, whether the stage of performance is a basketball court, a bobsleigh track, an advertising agency, or a medical school, everyone at that level will have a great shot on the basketball court, will have what would be considered the ideal combination of strength and speed for effectively pushing a bobsleigh, will have an amazingly creative mind for out-of-the-box thinking, or will be brilliantly smart in human sciences. You're not going to find someone in medical school who is *not* smart, although the variation of that intelligence will, as I see it, vary by that 10 percent.

So, you ask, what exactly makes up that 90 percent? That's the mental game. And the magnitude of your success depends on it. Sure, innate natural strengths play a role in success, but the key to excellence—what makes up the variance in that 90 percent—in *any* occupation or industry is not the ability to run fast or do mathematical equations quickly in your head. The difference is mental toughness. Performance output is determined by one's ability to *execute* the 10 percent, which is influenced by the thoughts and beliefs running through one's mind.

So far, Part Three: Own Your Story has been all about the power of positive thinking, about the attitude, habits, and mindset you need to adopt to ensure that you reach your real potential. It's been about digging deep within yourself not only to imagine greater things for yourself than you ever dreamed possible but also to believe that you're capable of them and propelling yourself forward to achieve those big dreams and goals. What it all boils down to is that for the journey to your best self, you need a healthy dose of mental toughness. To execute all your plans and goal-setting, and to overcome all the obstacles along the way, you need to be able to recognize what you can and can't control in a situation and concentrate on the things you can control. Your path to your personal excellence requires intentionality, discipline, grit, a positive outlook, and a laser-like focus on what it is you want to achieve.

A lot of variables are out of an athlete's control. But I chose to pursue Olympic goals anyway, knowing that I could very well *not* achieve them. I loved the challenge. So I chose to focus on the things that *were* in my control—my attitude, perspective, preparation, equipment, and so on. I chose to discover how good *I* could be—not how good I could be in relation to others. It wasn't about winning. It was about competing.

There is a big difference between *expecting* to succeed and knowing you are *capable* of succeeding. Believing that an outcome is guaranteed is much different than believing that it is *possible*. When asked if I expected to win in Vancouver or Sochi, the answer is no. Now, don't get me wrong—I also didn't expect to lose either. But expectations can be very dangerous. All I knew was that we possessed all the skills and abilities needed to win as long as we executed them properly and to the best of our abilities. I knew were *capable* of winning. We knew it was *possible*. So that meant focusing on *us*, what *we* were capable of, and not getting caught up and distracted by *other* factors. At that moment, it all boiled down to our ability to perform to the best of our abilities. *Execution.* Actually doing what we set out to do and trained so hard to accomplish. And the quality of execution comes down to mental toughness—focusing on what you can control to put your dreams into action and rise to your potential.

Focusing on others—their strengths and resources, their advantages—is toxic to performance. It only makes you anxious by thinking of the things you perceive to be lacking. Focusing on yourself—improving your skills, beating your own records, keeping a healthy mindset and perspective— empowers you to embrace the challenge, to see how good *you* can be. Focusing on what *you* can control is the ideal way to keep distractions and obstacles in check and perform at your absolute best.

Easier said than done, but sometimes a subtle shift in attitude can help to shut out the noise, relieving the pressure and expectations of others enough to allow you to focus on you and what you need to do. Earlier, I spoke of shifting your perspective from looking at doing laundry as something that *has* to be done to something that you *want* to do because of what it would lead to—your *root why*. Well, that technique of simply changing the vocabulary we use can also be applied to reduce the stress and anxiety we feel during situations we perceive to be high-pressure ones or to be out of our control. Changing vocabulary can help to put things in perspective. From 'have to' to 'want to' makes a big difference in how our brains perceive situations and, therefore, how our physiology reacts. And it helps to shift us from a negative mindset that sees only obstacles to a positive mindset that puts us in control of the situation, allowing us to focus on the task at hand.

At the Vancouver Olympics, just before our fourth and final run down the bobsleigh track, Kaillie and I were sitting in the start house at the top of the track in first place. You could cut the tension with a knife. We *couldn't* screw up on the last run. We were on home soil, in front of thousands of Canadians, and being watched by millions. They were counting on us. It was easy to feel the excitement, anticipation, and hopeful pressure of *millions* of people on us. We couldn't let them down. We *had* to win. We *needed* to have a good last run.

I turned to Kaillie and said, "Okay, we can leave now." She looked at me as though I had three heads and said, "What are you talking about? We still have our last run to do."

I quietly said, "Yes. But we *can* leave. We don't *have* to do the last run. We don't *have* to get a start record. We don't *have* to get a track record. We don't *have* to try to win this race... But we *want* to get a start record. We *want* to get a track record. We *want* to do this last run to try to win this race. We don't *have* to do anything. But we *want* to."

Can you see how that simple change in vocabulary helps in shifting perspective and, therefore, shifting the pressure? You don't *have* to do laundry. You *want* to do laundry because of your *root why*. We didn't *have* to perform our best on the last run to win at the Vancouver Olympics. We *wanted* to. And as soon as we reminded ourselves of that, the pressure that we felt from others suddenly took a back seat, and we were focused on executing well because, well... we *wanted* to.

As you may have realized by now, being able to shift perspective is a key ingredient to achieving success, particularly when it means seeing the positive in any situation, regardless of how dire it seems. If Kaillie and I were going to have any chance of winning, we were going to have to keep things in perspective and focus on *us* and the things in our control. Suddenly, we no longer felt the pressure not to fail; we saw the challenge to succeed. And had the mental toughness to go for it.

12

IMPACT

Realize Your Sphere
of Influence

THROUGHOUT THIS BOOK, I've been talking about your potential and what it takes to achieve *way more* than you ever thought possible. Part Three, in particular, has been inwardly focused, to help you cultivate the attitude and mental toughness that will empower you to go beyond what you thought you were capable of. But the fact is, you don't live in isolation. Just as the people around you have an effect on you, *you* have an impact on them.

What am I talking about? Well, we all influence others, no matter what. Whether we want to or not. Whether we realize it or not. Everything we do and choose affects other people. Somebody is watching the choices we make—the words we use, the actions we take. It could be a boss, a co-worker, a teammate, a parent, a neighbour, a friend, a child. We may not see, know, or understand the extent of our impact on others, but the ability to influence is not limited to athletes, movie stars, politicians, or others in the public eye. Someone is witnessing the choices we are making. A role model is simply a person of influence. And *you* have influence. Which means that *you* are a role model.

You have the power to inspire, motivate, and influence the people around you. Not with money or gifts, though those can all be nice gestures, but with your choices—your words and your actions.

That's the ultimate reason why I do what I do and share my experiences and perspectives. I have been lucky enough, and determined enough, to discover my own potential and go for the gold, literally and figuratively. And I have been lucky enough that others saw that potential in me even before I did and helped me recognize it. In the process, I have come to see that my own words and actions reach beyond me. They can inspire others and, in turn, help others believe in the possibilities of *their* life and discover what *they* are truly capable of. People are hungry for inspiration. That's why so many people are glued to their TVs during the Olympics—to see people doing seemingly remarkable things.

I have also realized that my impact on others is not merely about the medals around my neck, or even that I have those medals. Just like everyone, my impact on others comes from my actions, which are bound in my character, and my medals have simply given me a platform—they have afforded me a bigger stage from which I can, I hope, positively influence other people whom I normally wouldn't have reached and make a beneficial difference in the world. To me, this is what it means to live up to my own true potential, over and above my athletic achievements on the world stage.

Many other people have had an impact on my life; with their help and insight, I was able to tap into my athletic potential, which then, in turn, increased my own potential for affecting others.

So when I receive the compliment of being an inspiration and a positive role model, I am reminded of all the people who affected me in *my* life. Not just my parents and siblings, and not just my teachers and coaches, but neighbours, classmates, and even strangers. I often try to remind people, especially parents, that *they*, in fact, have more of an impact on the lives of their children and the people around them than any kind of celebrity does. *They* are the ones whose actions are seen daily, and whose words are heard every day. *They* are the ones instilling beliefs in the subconscious minds of their children. *They* have the biggest influence—not the celebrities being followed on social media. *You*, therefore, parent or not, should understand that you have influence. You have more influence than you think you do. And *you* can make a bigger impact than you ever could have imagined.

WE HAVE ALL had people influence our lives, sometimes without realizing the extent of that influence ourselves, and often without the other person even recognizing the impact they made.

When I was in grade seven, my family took a train to Ontario to spend Christmas with some relatives. Through my twelve-year old lens, it was a great holiday. I was too young and self-absorbed with my cousins to notice the underlying current of concern or the shadow of distraction behind my parents' eyes.

On the train back to Prince Edward Island after the holidays, my dad sat me down in our little cabin and told me that he had a brain tumour and he was going to Chicago the following March for brain surgery to have it removed. My one question at the time (although many more questions followed in the weeks to come) was, "What's the worst-case scenario? Could you die?" My dad knew that I would need to know so I wouldn't be blindsided. So he answered truthfully.

"Yes."

But, like any physician (and, I would like to think, any parent) would, my dad followed up the truth with a qualification to put things into perspective: "There is always the risk of death when it comes to any kind of surgery." And he explained a bit more as to why he *needed* to take that risk: "The tumour is quite large and is pushing on parts of my brain; that is causing some problems and will cause even more problems unless it can be removed. If it's not removed, then I will definitely die."

At the time, all I could say was "Okay." And I'm sure we all cried (although I can't clearly remember that part).

I'll tell you when I *definitely* cried. The more I learned about the brain at university, the more I realized how serious Dad's situation had been. At the age of twelve, it's hard to really grasp what the loss of a parent would be like or how that would affect the rest of your life. But when I studied Dad's surgery for a seminar presentation I had to do for one of my neuro courses at the University of Waterloo, it all hit home. Dad had given written permission to the hospital in Chicago for me to get access to all the doctor's notes and MRI images associated with his surgery so I could prepare my assignment.

Everyone is a role model to someone. Not *can be. Is.* It is your choice as to what kind of role model you want to be.

As I read through the notes, the more I realized how close I had *really* been to losing my father, not to mention the dozens of other complications that could have occurred.

The tumour was the size of a large orange (or small grapefruit), and although it was benign, the sheer size of it was causing neurological problems by pushing on brain tissue that wasn't supposed to be pushed on. The biggest problem was that it was pushing on the brain stem, squishing it to the point where it was almost completely pinched. The doctors suspected the tumour had been growing for at least eleven years before it was discovered, and if it continued to grow, which it most likely would, the brain stem would, undoubtedly, be pinched off, cutting off all neurological transmission to the rest of his body, including his respiratory function. Meaning: Dad would eventually die anyway without the surgery. It would just be a matter of time. So why not try?

But doctors in Canada wouldn't perform the surgery. Usually when something significant is discovered (like a tumour), the hospital that discovers it takes responsibility for it. But the hospital in this case didn't feel equipped or capable to handle a surgery of this magnitude. And, although they sent documentation of Dad's case to doctors and hospitals across the country, nobody wanted to take on something that seemed inoperable—something that was unlikely to have a positive outcome.

Finally, a doctor practising in the United States by the name of Ossama Al-Mefty agreed to do the surgery. And, thankfully, Dr. Al-Mefty had pioneered the skull-base surgery that my dad needed.

Sounds good, doesn't it? Well, prior to any neurosurgery, patients must undergo pre-op tests to ensure that if something goes wrong during surgery, the patient won't have a stroke on the table. In the brain, we all have what is called the circle of Willis, a circular system of arteries that sits at the base of the brain and supplies blood to all the different areas of the brain. It is designed so that if one section of the circle of Willis is affected (for example, if there is a brain bleed during surgery, and the surgeon has to clamp off a section), then blood can still be supplied to all areas of the brain by taking a different route in the system.

Unfortunately, during the pre-op tests, they discovered that my dad's circle of Willis was not functioning perfectly—that if an arterial section of his brain had to be clamped in an emergency during surgery, he would have a stroke on the operating table.

Not good.

Dr. Al-Mefty told all this to my parents the night before the scheduled surgery. The risks had increased. A lot. There were now just many more things that could go wrong if they went ahead with the operation.

I can only imagine what was going on in the minds and hearts of the three people in that hospital room.

Now, remember, my dad was also a physician, so he knew what the doctor must be going through. That meant he also knew what would happen if he did *not* have the surgery; it would just be a matter of time. A waiting game. He told Dr. Al-Mefty that he knew what the risks were, that he knew the doctors and nurses would do their best, that he knew there were no guarantees, and that he was willing to take the chance, whatever minuscule chance that may be.

That night, before leaving that room, Dr. Al-Mefty, a Muslim by religion, prayed with my Christian parents. It was not about religion. Whether you believe in God, Allah, or the collective energy of the human spirit, it was about the power of connection and the compassion of the human spirit. In a world where there is so much turmoil and lack of understanding when it comes to differences, even just *hearing* about that shared moment had a lasting impact on me, not to mention the impact it had on my parents.

The next day, Dr. Al-Mefty performed the surgery—a sixteen-hour ordeal.

And I am, and will forever be, grateful to him for his courage.

> **How often does your uncertainty about an outcome prevent you from tapping into your potential and testing your abilities?**

And how often does that prevent you from being able to make a positive impact on those around you? That's right—you have no idea!

Perspective. Isn't it amazing?!

Because of a letter that my sister sent with my mother, written for the surgeon who would be operating on her father—not just an anonymous patient—Dr. Al-Mefty called my sister before the surgery. And because of *that* phone call, my sister pursued a career in medicine to be able to have a similar impact on others. You really have no idea how far the impact of your actions and words will go.

To this day, I have never met Dr. Al-Mefty, but he has had a huge impact on my life. I feel a profound and overwhelming sense of gratitude toward him, hard to put into words. I have always wanted to meet him not because of the numerous prestigious awards he has won over the years for his contribution to neurological medicine (although that, in and of itself, is pretty amazing), but because of the impact he unknowingly has had on me (and my family as a whole). I want to thank him in person for not only what *he* did, but also for the impact that my *dad* has had on my life, which never would have happened had Dr. Al-Mefty not had the courage to step outside his comfort zone and believe in the possibilities of what he was capable of.

Now I mentor people on how to make things happen in their lives. I encourage them not to put off the things that are truly important to them. While that's all pretty amazing, I need to continue to heed my own words. So *I* am making a commitment to meet Dr. Ossama Al-Mefty in person within the next year (by the end of 2018) and will write about (or video doc) that meeting! (Stay tuned!)

We are all capable of *way more* than we give ourselves credit for, including our ability to affect those around us, have an impact on our communities, and make a positive difference in the world.

Impact and the Ripple Effect of Action

You don't have to be a parent or work in a profession that involves helping people—therapist, doctor, teacher, and so on—to have an impact on others. The words of a co-worker, a note from a friend, the random act of kindness from a stranger can all have a powerful influence on your life. We are affected not only by what we experience directly but also by what we witness and are exposed to. Doing one random act of kindness will not only impact the recipient but will also impact those who witness it, those who hear about it, and those who *feel* it when those people choose to pay it forward in their own lives.

Think about it: Knowing that there are good people out there in the world doing good things for others, defying odds, making a positive difference despite their circumstances... it shifts our mood, doesn't it? It gives us a positive energy that we then carry with us, making our hearts lighter and our subsequent interactions with others much brighter and more pleasant than they may have been otherwise.

I call this the 'ripple effect of action'. Think of a pebble being dropped into water. You can picture this water in a bucket, or you can picture a calm lake with a mirror-like surface. Either way, when a pebble is dropped into the water, it makes an impact, and you will notice a ripple effect—mini waves that form a ring around the point of impact that ripple outwards from that very spot. This is a metaphor for our actions. Good or bad actions have a ripple effect, and it's virtually impossible to determine the definite end point of those actions. But because I want to make this world a better place, I will focus on the good actions—the good deeds—that make a positive difference not only in some*one's* life but also in the larger world because of the continual ripple effect from those actions. My actions affect your life, and your actions, in turn, affect other lives, and so on and so on. We all need to be aware of the tremendous potential impact we are having and choose to make that impact as positive as possible.

INSPIRED BY CHARACTER

In 1988, when I was ten years old, Barb McNeill, my swimming instructor, set her mind to swimming across the English Channel as a personal goal. If successful, she would be the first person from Atlantic Canada to do so, and only the fifteenth of all Canadians to do the classic marathon swim. On August 24, 1989, when I was eleven, she accomplished the feat—the goal she had set for herself.

But the fact that she was successful at doing something that so few people have ever done is not the part of her story that continues to influence me to this day.

After 17.5 hours of swimming, Barb was pulled from the water with only four kilometres to go because of strong currents. But she did not give up. She hadn't trained so hard to let her goal go so easily. So, one week later, Barb set out again to tackle this amazing challenge of hers with renewed drive and determination.

This time the swim was going well, but with less than five kilometres to go to reach the French shores—her goal within reach—Barb *voluntarily* left the water to help another swimmer who had suffered a heart attack nearby. She knew her skills in resuscitation as a swimming instructor and lifeguard could potentially save a life, and she chose to help someone in need over achieving her own goal.

Although Barb did, in fact, conquer the English Channel the following year after a seventeen-hour gruelling swim through engulfing waves, and I am extremely happy for her (just as I am for anyone who achieves a hard-earned goal), it is the *sacrifice* of her own goal—the voluntary denial of success the previous year—that has had a lasting effect on me over the years. The choice she made with no consideration to the enormous amount of time and energy spent training; the possible loss of opportunity to attempt her goal again; the judgments of sponsors, supporters, naysayers. Just an authentic choice that she would not regret in the long run. The *right* choice for her! And I admire her for that; for her uncompromising ethics, despite the pull of success right around the corner (or over the next wave, in this case).

Barb's story of grit—passion and perseverance –has had a big impact on me. The *ripple effect* of her actions has stayed with me forever—putting someone else's needs above her own wants. That's perspective. Barb McNeill—her work ethic, determination, and character—is someone to be admired. The epitome of a great role model.

MY PARENTS INSTILLED in me and my siblings the belief in opportunities and possibilities, which I truly *believed*, in combination with a positive mindset, hard work, and perseverance, was all one needed to achieve their heart's desire. And I still do.

But that belief was challenged when I worked in Trinidad and Tobago as a Disability Sports Program Officer with the Special Education Unit from October 2001 to July 2002, and

I suddenly realized how naive I was when I was faced with people with disabilities that far exceeded anything I'd worked with before. To me, at the time, I saw these people as having limited possibilities. In my role, I was considered to be somewhat of an expert, and yet I was the one who was taught a lesson. It took one young boy to show me that my limited beliefs existed only because of the assumptions I had adopted from society.

As part of my job, I moved around to different schools for kids with physical and developmental disabilities. I was at one of those schools for a Christmas pageant when a boy dressed as Joseph approached me. It wasn't hard to see why he was in a school for children with physical disabilities: he walked on his toes because his ankles were fused. In fact, *all* the joints in his legs and his arms—except for his wrists, which were very stiff—somehow seemed to be fused. He didn't appear to have any bend in his elbows or knees.

That was before I even knew about occupational therapy, or had any experience or deeper understanding of situations like these, and part of me wondered what, I think, anyone would: What do you do with a kid like that? How do you integrate him with the others?

Then, at the pageant, still dressed as Joseph, he stood behind the steelpan, a kind of steel drum that originates from Trinidad and Tobago, and, with arms outstretched, began to play the most beautiful music. He was remarkable.

The next time I saw that same boy was at the school's sports day. Even though I had seen him play the steelpan, I had reservations about what he would be able to do athletically. He'd signed up for cricket. They put him out to bowl (the cricket equivalent of pitching).

And, again, he was remarkable.

For those of you unfamiliar with the sport of cricket, all you need to know for the sake of this story is that you're not *supposed* to bend your arm when you bowl. The best bowlers in the world have little-to-no bend in their elbow and a wide arc windmill motion. As a result, the boy was, in fact, better than most kids of *any* age, even those without any disability whatsoever. He blew me away.

This kid was different. This kid was extreme. And that the severity of his condition did not keep him down showed me how to see new possibilities I had not considered before. Seeing his potential required me to see his difference on its own terms, not mine. I had to stop looking at what he *wouldn't* be able to do and start looking at what he *would* be able to do—I had to change my perspective to see his *abilities,* not his disabilities.

In showing me what he was capable of, this boy made me realize what we are *all* capable of. Or, at least, that we are certainly capable of *way more* than we usually ever attempt or even imagine. Without realizing his impact, that boy made me realize how many excuses so many of us make to rationalize and justify not doing things.

My experiences in Trinidad and Tobago and my deep-rooted passion for working with people less fortunate—most often people with disabilities—led me to pursue my master's degree in occupational therapy. I wanted to help others who were facing problems to see their situations from a different perspective, to find solutions instead of obstacles. I wanted to be the catalyst that would help them embrace the *challenge* of seeing what they were still capable of, despite their less-than-ideal circumstances. When trying to help a client achieve a goal, occupational therapists will look for ways to improve the person's physical, mental, or emotional abilities, to see if they can improve the environment in which the activity takes place; and they will also see if there are, perhaps, different ways of doing the same thing, or getting the same thing (emotional experience) *out* of an activity.

What I loved about being an occupational therapist was that I could help shift my clients' perspective to see their situation, however seemingly grim, from a different point of view, help them identify what was truly important to them, and help them break down their goals into manageable and achievable steps with the intention of getting them back to doing the activities (*occupations*) they most valued. It was about inspiration and motivation, and helping them see the possibilities that still existed within the parameters of their circumstance.

I am asked quite frequently if I can see myself ever going back to work as an occupational therapist. For me, it was truly a rewarding occupation. But now? As a speaker and mentor, I get to have that kind of impact on rooms full of people. I am coaching people beyond the perceived obstacles that stand in their way to achieving their goals. I am still doing what occupational therapists do—enabling people to see the potential that exists within them and to strive to fulfill it; helping people tap into their potential and to discover what they are truly capable of.

The Power of Words

Although 'actions speak louder than words', as the saying goes, it does not mean that words don't have power. We've already seen that words can be used to lift someone up or drag someone down. They can be used to de-motivate (a strategy used by lobsters and naysayers), or they can serve as a tool of inspiration, motivation, and empowerment.

The Canadian women's hockey team was playing for gold against the United States the night after we won our gold medal at the Sochi Olympics in 2014. Kaillie and I had been up most of the night doing media interviews and were back again the next morning to do more. To save time, they put Kaillie and me in different rooms to accommodate all the reporters most efficiently. Which is why I wasn't with Kaillie when I came out of an interview and was approached by a gentleman I did not know.

"Hi, Heather. My name is So-and-So [I don't actually remember his name]. I do mostly hockey reporting, and I want to tell you something that I think you'd find really interesting."

Okay...

"I was just speaking with Caroline Ouellette [the captain of the Canadian women's hockey team], and I asked her what she had said—what words of inspiration she had said—to her team last night before their gold medal game tonight. Well, she just looked at me and said, 'Oh, I didn't have to say anything.' 'I'm sorry?' I replied. 'As a captain, you didn't say anything to your team?' And she said, 'No, I didn't have to say anything to get them inspired and pumped up. We just all got together as a team in the athletes lounge and watched our women's bobsled team win their race!'"

I couldn't help but smile.

And then the reporter added, "You know... I might be seeing them later, if you want to write them a note... "

Now, I would never want to throw anyone off their game by doing something or contributing something that was not part of their normal preparation or routine, but Kaillie and

I both knew a number of the women on the team, and I also knew that if I *did* send a note, it would go to someone who could make the decision as to whether it was appropriate or not to give it to the team. So, I wrote:

> *Girls, there are ups and downs in every race and game, but we are proof that if you keep believing in the possibilities, results can be golden. Own it! The ice is yours! Fight until the bitter end!*
>
> *Smiles...*
>
> *Heather and Kaillie*

That night, the team faced a significant deficit like Kaillie and I had in our race: they were down 2-0 with ten minutes to go in the game. Although many people watching the game gave up on them, *they* didn't. They came back to tie the game, and then won Olympic gold in overtime.

I found out later that Hayley Wickenheiser had read that note to the players before their game, and then taped it to a locker beside the door. Of course, I'm not saying that's why they *won* or anything... ☺

I'm just kidding! They won on their own! And that note may not have played any part in their win whatsoever. But it *is* interesting to consider where people find that extra bit of inspiration, where *you* find it, and where *you* can perhaps provide it for others, keeping them focused on the possibilities... a note, an email, a few encouraging words, or a phone call to a teammate, a co-worker, a neighbour, a friend, or a family member. Perhaps even a stranger. Words *are* powerful. You never know how far-reaching a few thoughtful words can go, or the extent of the impact they will make. Maybe the 'ripple effect' from that note I wrote will mean that other notes of inspiration have been, and will continue to be, passed on to other people.

Everything You Do Matters

The question I am asked most often about my Olympic experiences is "Which gold medal is my favourite?" That's right. It's about my medals. People want to know if I like the Vancouver one or the Sochi one better.

That may seem like a relatively easy question to answer because they look so different, but it's not. I tend to bounce back and forth because of the vastly different circumstances surrounding each victory.

The 2010 Vancouver medal is special because we were not only underdogs going into those Games but also competing on home soil. To win when you aren't expected to is one thing. To win on home soil, for me however, is a feeling that can *never* be replicated—a feeling that lies much deeper than words.

But, as I mentioned, when we arrived in Sochi four years later, expectations were high. Kaillie and I were there as defending Olympic champions, and, historically, successfully defending that medal seemed highly unlikely. So, to defend our medals successfully under that kind of pressure was a pretty amazing feeling. Not to mention proving to people that I could actually make it there despite having had hip surgery so close to the Games.

Although I keep bouncing back and forth to answer that question based on circumstance, I keep being drawn back to the Vancouver medal itself. What makes the Vancouver medal so special goes beyond circumstance and results—for *anyone* in those Games, not just me. Every Olympic host country creates its own look for its Games medals. The Royal Canadian Mint spent two-and-a-half years designing the 2010 medals to make history and an extraordinary statement about the world as a whole.

For the first time ever, the medals were not flat. They are wavy to reflect the mountainous topography of British Columbia. But look at all the medals next to one another and you will see they are not just wavy but each one is *different*. In fact, the designs on the front of *all 615 medals* created for the Vancouver Games are unique! Every one of them has a different design on the front—even those given out to members of the same team.

The reason behind this goes beyond a desire for each medal to be special. It is a statement about connection: when all 615 medals slightly overlap one another, the unique designs combine to form one big First Nations design based on the orca whale.

The idea behind the medals being created in this way is that every Olympic medallist is forever connected in some way—that we share something special. We competed in different sports, on different surfaces, and against different competitors, but we were all able to reach the podium in whatever our pursuit. The distinctive design on the front of *each* medal reflects the fact that each of us has a completely different story—a different journey, different background, different motivation for doing what we did. We experienced different things, grew up in different support systems, and made different choices to get to that podium. We faced different challenges and overcame different obstacles along the way, and will all, most likely, choose to do different things with our successes. Yet, we are all connected—indeed, *united*—by what we were able to accomplish.

What a great message we can all take to heart in living our lives every day. We are connected as much by what makes us unique as what makes us the same. We may be united by a company, school, team, ethnicity, nationality, hometown... but we all have completely different stories.

Different stories... and yet connected—intertwined by the ripple effect of our actions. Not only do we have the power to change the direction of our story—how our stories end— crafted by the choices we make from this point on, but we also have the power to impact the stories of others simply by how we choose to live our lives. *We* get to choose the design of our lives, which will, in turn, impact the overall *design* of the world.

This impact can be on our environment, the people around us, our communities, *and* on the world as a whole, simply by the choices we make and the paths we take.

In addition to being a motivational speaker, I chose to brave the wind and the extreme cold to climb Mount Vinson in Antarctica because, ultimately, I thought it would make a big positive impact not only on our war veterans but also on those who hear of the expedition and its cause. What I didn't expect was the huge impact the expedition had on me.

Before heading out on the excursion, the team shared their stories and their reasons for doing this challenging climb. One of the businesspeople on the expedition explained that a friend had first told him about the trip. And when he discussed it with his wife at home—the time commitment, the training involved, the conditions and possible risks of the expedition itself—his daughter looked up from her homework and said quite plainly, "Why don't you just write them a cheque?"

That simple question bothered him. It got him thinking. Why *wouldn't* he just write a cheque? His daughter's simplistic and almost dismissive comment hit a nerve with him. Would simply writing a cheque be as effective? Certainly the money would be a help to the charity organizing the trek, but would it make as big an *impact*? Would it make as big an impact on *him*? Would he really *feel* any differently about it? I mean, writing a cheque wouldn't make waves in his life—wouldn't put any kind of obvious dent in his bank account. So, would it help? Yes. Would it make as big an impact? No. Had his daughter not mentioned so indifferently the option of writing a cheque, that's probably exactly what he would have done. Instead, he committed to the challenge, to action, and *chose* to make an impact on himself. *And* on his daughter.

For *me,* ultimately, the pull of the challenge was too strong and the cause too great to refuse the opportunity. And what I got in return was something even greater than I imagined. Another shift in perspective.

A number of people were quite emotional upon returning to High Camp after having summited the 16,050-foot mountain, conquering something so physically and mentally challenging. But I was pretty composed, being somewhat accustomed to that feeling of physical and mental accomplishment, until one of the soldiers came up to me, gave me a big hug, and said quietly in my ear, "Thank you." *What?* "Thank you for doing what you do, and helping to raise awareness. And thank you for taking the time to be here and allowing us the chance to do this."

I broke from the hug to look at him and say, "You are thanking *me*? Thank *you*, thank you, *thank you*." And I just lost it. I couldn't stop crying for half an hour. I wouldn't take my goggles off until I had stopped, making it impossible to wipe away the tears.

I don't think I'd ever been *emotional* about accomplishing a physical feat before. Only twice had I ever jumped up and down with excitement from winning a bobsleigh race, and both were come-from-behind victories that were *highly unlikely*. But the emotion I felt in that moment at High Camp had nothing to do with accomplishing the tough physical feat of having summited a mountain, nor was it the beauty of where we were that overwhelmed me and affected me to the core. Yes, I had done something outside of my comfort zone, which I was pleased about. But the emotion had to do with impact: the impact that I had made on others by choosing to take on that challenge, but more so with the tremendous impact that the experience and people had *on me*. I was profoundly touched by the personal stories of the servicemen and -women I met, several of whom climbed despite physical and psychological injuries they had suffered in battle, like Sergeant Thomas White.

Sometimes when you think you're making an impact on a cause or on those around you, it is, in fact, they who make the most profound impact on you. There is no way to predict the extent to which our actions have an impact in this world, so choose your actions—and your words—wisely, as the role model you are. Because *everything* you do matters.

CONCLUSION

BELIEVE IN THE *POSSIBILITIES*

CANNOT SAY WITH absolute certainty that you will achieve your goals. But pursuing any dream or goal is not about the guarantees. It's about the possibilities! There *are* no guarantees in sports, business, or life. But believing in the *possibilities* allows you to challenge your preconceived boundaries and test not only the threshold of your potential but also the threshold of what is possible. Imagine what your life could look like if you chose to *own* it: own your choices, embrace challenges, and refuse to make or accept excuses while in pursuit of the life you've dreamed of. Imagine how far you could go. Imagine...

Then start actually *believing*. And then *plan*. And then *pursue*. Take a step. Move away from excuses toward your potential. Make an impact on this world by living to inspire—because you are living the life you want and deserve.

With the abundance of self-help books and other tools out there addressing a myriad of obstacles to overcome, what's missing? What do people need first and foremost in order to implement all the advice that's available to them but will never be applied? *Belief.* People will not change their behaviour—implement any kind of self-improvement suggestions, even if they are brilliant ones—if they don't first *believe* that the desired outcome is possible. How often do you hear people say, "What's the point?" Perhaps the voice in *your* head is saying the same thing to you.

That's when you need a shift in perspective. Think about the most optimistic person you know. It can be someone you know personally, or it can be a celebrity you see on TV, or... it can be me. Last year I attended a professional speakers conference, and just as I was heading to the final dinner, a woman saw me come around the corner and she suddenly burst into tears. She explained to me that she, her husband, and her teenaged daughter had heard me speak the year before. Just a few months before this conference, her daughter—being recruited to play varsity volleyball the following year—slipped on a bobby pin on the volleyball court, severely injured her knee, and had to have emergency surgery. After the procedure, the doctors told her that she'd never be able to play volleyball again. After they left her hospital room, she looked at her mother and said that she didn't want to talk to anyone else about what she could or could *not* do unless it was Heather Moyse. What a compliment, what an honour! What a chance to have an impact on someone's life.

Did I tell her that she would play volleyball again? No, of course not. But that wasn't the point. We discussed the possibilities that existed, other opportunities in her life, *and* the perspective of embracing the *challenge* to see how far she could get in terms of rehabilitation and returning to the sport she loved. If that's what she decided she wanted. The point was that, after we talked, she believed in the *possibilities* again.

I want you to shift your perspective and discover a whole new world of possibilities.

IN JUNE 2016, I was fortunate to have been invited as a special guest of the Canadian contingent to attend the Invictus Games in Orlando, Florida. These Games are the epitome of what I believe: we are all capable of *way more* than what we give ourselves credit for. The Invictus Games were started by Prince Henry of Wales (a.k.a. Prince Harry) to reflect and express the unconquerable character of wounded, injured, and sick servicemen and -women. The Invictus Games mission is to "harness the power of sport to inspire recovery, support rehabilitation and generate a wider understanding and respect for those who serve their country".

I attended several events and competitions that week, and, although having been trained as an occupational therapist and having worked with people with disabilities before, those Games still had a huge impact on me.

I knew all along that these brave men and women were capable of physical feats like the ones I saw at the Invictus Games. But I think some of them surprised themselves! This was an opportunity for them to realize what they could, *potentially,* be capable of, not just in sports but in their every-day lives as well, despite having lost a limb, the *use* of their limb(s), or the psychological trauma that had overshadowed their lives. What I saw over and over again at the Invictus Games was eyes opened, potential recognized, and a sense of self renewed. Ever since my experience of living and working in Trinidad and Tobago, I have believed that sports are an ideal medium for development between and within nations, within communities, and within individuals—a way to reveal to people, including those in transition or facing monumental personal challenges, what they are capable of.

But I witnessed more than physical potential and outright abilities. It was the crazy courage and undeniable heart and empathy of the competitors that impacted me more than anything else.

I watched an athlete on the Canadian team, a single-leg amputee, struggle through the 100 and the 200 metres and finish both in last place. But when another participant, who had crossed the finish line well ahead of him, collapsed at the end of the 200 from exhaustion, the Canadian racer, also utterly exhausted, rushed straight over, held out a hand, and helped him up long before anyone else even noticed the man was down.

I watched a women's wheelchair 100-metre sprint. Long after the winners crossed the finish line, I heard a gradual escalation of cheering from the stands closer to where the race had started, and I became aware of a woman from Jordan who was still coming down the track. As she slowly wheeled down the straightaway, fighting to move her chair forward, all the racers who had finished gathered at the finish line, watching, cheering, and screaming encouragement, just as loudly as the people in the stands were chanting, "Jordan! Jordan!" Turns out, she had never been in a racing wheelchair before, and they are much different to manoeuvre than a regular wheelchair. The cheers from the entire crowd were louder for her when she crossed the finish line than for the medallists, and the joyful noise included applause and cheers from the medallists themselves.

I watched a distance wheelchair race—probably one or two laps of the track—in which one athlete was well ahead of another, whose chair was seemingly not working properly. But instead of crossing the finish line, the athlete in the lead turned around and headed back down the track, circling behind the other athlete and pushing him forward with his own wheelchair all the way to the finish line. Just metres before they reached the finish, the athlete being pushed peeled out to the side, allowing the other racer (and, in his opinion, the rightful winner of the race) to cross the line first.

These are people who make me want to achieve more, literally push me to climb mountains. They remind me to keep tracking my purpose, my *why*, from the days I am standing on mountaintops right down to the days I just don't feel like going to 'work'.

As I've mentioned, I almost walked away from bobsledding until my dad helped me to *come from away*, to see things in a different way so I could discover my true purpose—my *root why*. And now I feel blessed to be able to do that for others. I know I never would have gotten to where I am today, wouldn't have achieved all I have, if he had not done that for me. I would have had an abundance of untapped potential inside me, talent I never would have discovered, impact I never would have made.

It's not too late to change your story from a fourth place to a podium finish or even to a gold-medal result based on *your* definition of what that means. I want you to shift your perspective, believe in the possibilities of what you can achieve, and realize that you are capable of *way more* than you currently give yourself credit for: not only your physical or mental abilities but your ability to have a positive impact on those around you, to make a difference in your community and in the world by your choices—your words and your actions. I want you to be open to opportunities, tap into your potential, and discover a whole new world of possibilities. I want you to take your life not only to the next level of success but more so to a higher level of fulfillment. I want you to be the person you *want* to be, and the person I *believe* you can be. *You* just have to believe it too.

> **Desired outcome: To look back on your journey—including all the choices you've made along the way— and, regardless of outcome, have no regrets.**

So I wish you not *luck* but *courage* to follow your *own* path—to make the choices that are perhaps not easy but are right for *you*. I wish for you the perspective to redefine 'realistic' and embrace challenges, and for the creativity, resiliency, and grit to overcome the obstacles along the path to your best self. And I wish for you the discovery of your *root why* to keep you 'rooted' in your purpose.

But most of all, I wish for you the *belief* that we are *all* capable of *way more* than we give ourselves credit for. Because although a goal may *seem* too big, and an outcome may *seem* highly unlikely, it is without a doubt still possible! Now it's your turn. Shift your perspective, seize your potential, and own your story.

Q & A

ALTHOUGH THE CONTENT in this Q & A doesn't necessarily fit with the messaging of the book, I added it
to answer some of the questions I get asked quite
frequently—just some interesting tidbits about my life both
in and out of sport.

How did you and Kaillie Humphries get paired up?

When I joined the Canadian National Bobsleigh Team in the
fall of 2005 and then competed five months later in the 2006
Winter Olympics in Torino, just like when anyone joins a new
team, I inadvertently took someone else's spot. In my case, it
was someone who had been training for years to compete in
those Olympic Games. That person was Kaillie Humphries,
my teammate with whom I was later able to win gold twice
for Canada.

That's right—Kaillie was a brakeman. And I took her spot.
And she didn't speak to me for the next couple of years! Until
we were on a road trip in Europe. Not the fun kind of road
trip you would do with friends on vacation; the kind that bobsleigh athletes have to take between our various competition

venues—anywhere from three to eleven hours of driving in passenger vans or cube vans with the sleds in the back.

To pass the time during these long drives, we'd sing to music, tell jokes (which didn't last very long), discuss movies we had just seen and attractive guys on other teams and who'd dated whom, and talk about home and family. Before leaving for the 2008–09 season, a friend had given me *The Book of Questions,* a pocketbook with a thousand questions (e.g., If you could have dinner with any three people, dead or alive, who would they be? If you were stranded on a deserted island, what two items could you not live without?). On this particular road trip, I was sitting behind Kaillie, who was driving the passenger van, and I was reading these questions out loud to my teammates, who were blurting out the answers.

Well, I suddenly read a question (and, no, unfortunately I was not reading them in my head first!) that asked something like: *If you could get back at someone from your past whom you felt had done you wrong, would you send them to . . .* And my voice trailed off as I realized how awkward the question was in that situation. I tried to laugh it off and said, "I'm probably somewhere in your top ten, aren't I, Kaillie?!" A long silence (and a look of *What did you do?* from two of the other women in the van). And then Kaillie finally said, "No. I've come to realize that what happened in Torino wasn't your fault—you were just doing your job."

I hadn't realized that I'd been carrying around that burden since those Games. Yes, in sports it's about the best competing, but it's not always easy knowingly taking someone else's spot. But at that moment, I suddenly felt lighter. That silly little book broke the ice, so to speak.

And good thing it did because a couple months later, in January 2009, the coaches asked me if I would push Kaillie in a race. After the Torino Olympics, Kaillie had decided to become a driver so she could never be bumped from a sled again. I felt that pushing her was a way I could give something back to Kaillie—something I felt partly responsible for taking from her three years earlier. I pushed her for that race and the next one. Our chemistry on the ice was undeniable. I pushed her for four of the last five races of the season, and then one year later we stood at the top of the Olympic podium in Vancouver together. And then four years after *that* we stood on top of the Olympic podium in Sochi together and had the honour of carrying our country's flag in the closing ceremony.

What's something about the sport of bobsledding that people probably wouldn't know?

Well, because bobsledding isn't something that many get to experience, there are a lot of factors people wouldn't necessarily be aware of. However, I will tell you about a few things...

1 **Brakemen can be switched in and out at any time.** The teams you see competing are very rarely, if ever, set in stone. The pilot's name is the team name (e.g., Team Upperton or Team Humphries), but the brakemen are interchangeable. The brakemen are often being tested and compared with one another throughout the whole season to determine which one will push a particular sled at the Olympics or the World Championships at the end of the season. If there is a brakeman who significantly stands out among the others, there's not as much need for constant testing, but he or she could still be switched out at any time. It's not easy being a brakeman, which is why many brakemen decide to become drivers (like Kaillie did), so they won't be switched out of the sled—they will always get to race.

2   **Brakemen don't actually brake during the race.** I'm often asked about how I know when to brake. Well, in my opinion, a good brakeman will know all the corners of the track before going down. So, basically, I just brake after we cross the finish line! People are often surprised by that answer, inevitably asking why we are called brakemen if we don't brake while going down the track. My answer is that 'pushers' just doesn't sound right as a title! ☺ As brakemen, our job is to get the sled going as fast as possible as quickly as possible at the start of the race. The start is always 50 metres long (between timing lights) with the grooves for the runners to slide in lasting only 35 metres, meaning we have to load into the sled before it goes out of the grooves. We have 35 metres to get a fast push-start and give the sled the fastest velocity possible going into the track. People watching races are usually only aware of the start times, but the velocities are just as important, if not *more* important, than the start times. Let me explain.

The whole race comes down to hundredths of a second, with your time starting at the top of the track. As brakemen, we are constantly trying to shave off a hundredth here and there by making small tweaks to a variety of factors: changing our hand positions on the handles, adjusting the depth we 'fall' into the sled at the beginning to get the best push off the starting block, and so on. The start time also comes down to how far a brakeman runs down the track. But that is a precarious component. As brakemen, we always want to be applying continuous force on the sled to move it forward, but there will be a moment at which the sled will match the brakeman's speed and then will start going faster than the brakeman. Running two steps (one cycle) too short won't give you the fastest start time. But running one cycle too far, although perhaps showing a faster start time, will have a slower velocity seeing as the brakeman, without realizing it, probably had to pull *back* on the handles to get in the sled. That slower velocity then affects the speed of the sled the whole way down the track.

Once we are in the sled, our job is not to screw anything up—to be as still as possible. There have been times when I jumped into the back of a sled and caught my foot so it wasn't positioned properly on the foot peg, but I knew we were already out of the grooves so if I moved I might jostle the sled (which is skidding on top of the ice surface on rounded runners, as opposed to ice skates, for example, that dig into the ice) and cause it to fishtail, losing some of the speed we gained at the beginning. Also, by knowing the direction of all the corners, brakemen can anticipate the abrupt movements of the sled and brace *against* those movements, preventing (or at least reducing) the possibility of banging against the sides of the sled. Those actions keep all the force moving forward, instead of anything being wasted on side-to-side movement.

3   **Bobsledding is not a glamorous sport.** People are surprised when they hear about what we have to do as high-performance bobsleigh athletes. If you think we just show up at a competition venue to warm up and race, you are mistaken. I'm not even referring to the off-season dry-land training. I'm talking about while we are *in* competition season on the World Cup circuit. *We* are the ones who transport our sleds in cube vans from venue to venue and load them (almost 180 kilograms/400 pounds for a women's sled) in and out. *We* do a lot of the sled work with the team mechanic (if/when there *is* a team mechanic). And *we* polish our own runners. What do I mean by that? Well,

each of the four runners is mounted in a vise attached lengthwise to the side of a table. Using a strip of sandpaper (about the length of an iPhone and the width of two fingers) resting flat in the palm of our hand and between the grooves of two of our fingers, we glide the sandpaper back and forth along the runner surface about twenty times per paper, removing scratches as we go. But seeing as sandpaper is scratchy and would itself leave behind fine marks on the runners, we do this same routine over and over again from a coarser-grit sandpaper all the way to the finest grit possible (which actually feels completely smooth). Touch-ups happen throughout the training week, but polishing runners before a race is a very tedious (but necessary!) job and can sometimes take a couple of hours to make them gleaming and race-ready.

People always talk about the importance of planning and being prepared, but that doesn't just mean preparing physically in terms of training. What are some examples of other ways you prepare for high performance?

Well, I'll give you three examples:

1   When I first arrived in Torino, at my first Olympic Games in February 2006, I went to the track to check out the situation. I looked at the big stands set up at the starting line and the finish line, and I took a moment to imagine them filled with people. I was also told there would be a big media camera running on a track *beside* us during our starts as we pushed and sprinted down the track before jumping in, so I took a moment to visualize what that would be like. I continued to do so over the next few days

until it was no longer a distraction when I thought about what I needed to do to perform at my best at the start. When our first day of racing finally arrived, I didn't even notice the camera was there.

2   The Canadian Olympic Committee (COC) anticipated a potential source of fatigue for the Canadian athletes during the Vancouver Olympics. The buildings in the Athletes Village that housed the Canadian athletes were the farthest away from the cafeteria tent. Not that it was extremely far, but even a fifteen-minute walk (each way) could add an additional hour of walking (or more if an athlete chose to eat breakfast there instead of in the Canadian lounge). This may not sound like very much to you, but elite athletes have trained their bodies in a certain way, and any deviation can put stress on their nervous system, which affects the speed at which their muscles fire. For me, an explosive sprint athlete in a sport that is won or lost by hundredths of a second, I needed my nervous system fresh and firing on all cylinders. So I was extremely grateful for the foresight of the COC to arrange to have bicycles for the athletes to use. Electric bikes!

3   Anyone who knows me well knows that I am not a 'dieter'. I do not restrict things in my diet, and I do love my moments of sugary bliss. But I also know what nutrients I need to perform well, so I make sure that I give my body what it needs. When you're on tour, it's not as easy to get the nutrients you need, or sometimes even the food you like, so you sometimes have to 'plan for performance'. For instance, I know that I don't enjoy European breakfasts. I'm not into croissants and cheese and cold cuts in

the morning. I also know how extremely greasy and plastic our North American breakfasts served in some hotel/ motel buffets can sometimes be. I wanted to be able to show up for a race and know, with certainty, that I didn't have to worry about the digestion of my food, feeling gross, or not having enough energy to perform. So I brought my breakfast with me. I ate Red River cereal *every* morning while I was on tour. And no, it's not a sponsor (although... maybe it *should* be!). ☺

Typically, if eating at home, I will cook the cereal on the stove, but I had to think about where I would be. So I also brought a large bowl, measuring cups, and a bag of brown sugar (to sprinkle on top). All I needed was a microwave, and then I didn't have to worry about whether or not I would have a good breakfast of substance before training or competing. Over the Christmas holidays, I contacted and confirmed with the COC that the Athletes Village would, in fact, include a microwave. One less thing I had to worry about when the time came.

You didn't follow the typical path leading toward representing your country in the sport of rugby. Tell us about that.

I almost didn't play rugby at all. In grade nine I had sprained my ankle so badly in basketball that it had to be put in a cast, so, although I *wanted* to play rugby like my older sister had, I was worried about getting injured and not being able to do all the *other* sports and activities I was involved in.

Mr. Turtle—the school's rugby coach at the time—made it quite clear that he wanted me to play. As I mentioned in an earlier chapter, he saw the potential in me before I did. But... I was pretty stubborn, and it took a lot of convincing.

He arranged for a substitute teacher (who wasn't at all bad-looking, which definitely helped inspire my grade-ten self) to take me aside and show me some tackling techniques, which made me realize two things: 1) how there is reason and structure behind all the seemingly unstructured 'madness' on the field, and 2) how much fun the game is!

I played rugby for three years in high school and during the last two years of my undergraduate degree at the University of Waterloo. Then I trained with a men's team that summer (2000) before playing with the National Women's Under-23 Rugby Team against the United States at the end of that summer. I lived and worked in Ireland for the first half of 2001, where I played for the Blackrock Rugby Club. I went back to P.E.I. for the summer of 2001 then went to Trinidad and Tobago that October. I found a rugby club within the first two weeks, although there wasn't really a women's league so, again, I trained mostly with the men. I then helped the club coach some girls who showed up for a rugby camp, and my role expanded. I was determined to grow the sport I love, and so every week the girls each needed to bring a new friend. When my internship ended, I was hired by the Trinidad and Tobago Rugby Football Union as a Women's Rugby Coach and Development Officer. Although I played in a couple of rugby sevens tournaments (one with a cast on my wrist), when I returned to Canada in the spring of 2004 I really hadn't played fifteens rugby (fifteen people a side versus seven people a side) since I was in Ireland in 2001.

My sister wanted me to play club rugby with her, saying that it would be fun to play together again, having previously done so for only one summer (1999) when we both played on the P.E.I. provincial team. And she was right: it *would* be fun. But... did I *really* want to put my body through all of that again?! The tackling?! Throwing myself to the ground?! But . . . it *would* be fun to play with her again . . .

So, I joined her. And the club coach just happened to be the Ontario provincial coach, so I found myself at the next (and last) tryout for the provincial team. And during the only game the Ontario team had prior to the Canadian Rugby Championships at the end of the summer, a national rugby coach just *happened* to be *there*! And I was suddenly invited to a development camp in Ottawa following nationals. And then I found myself starting my master's degree, already asking if it was possible to be away for two weeks that November to go to England with the National Senior Women's Rugby Team for my first tour—my first tour *and* my first try.

How did the unfortunate death of Georgian luge athlete Nodar Kumaritashvili at the Vancouver Olympic Games affect you?

Kaillie and I first heard the terrible news while we were driving from Whistler to Vancouver for the opening ceremony. I'm not sure it had really sunk in at the time, but over the next few days it was a thought that lingered in my mind. It wasn't the safety of the track that I questioned, or grief from having lost a friend (since I had never met him), but thoughts of my family that swam through my brain. I kept thinking of his family and of *my* family, and how awful it would be for *them* if something ever happened to me while doing something in which they supported me.

But I knew they would always support me in whatever I chose to pursue, and I continued to remind myself that we had already done a lot of training on that track—that we were experienced—but that crashing was always a risk and part of the sport.

That being said, there are people everywhere who are facing stress and emotional duress every day who still have to get up in the mornings and go to work—they have to execute what they have been trained to do, regardless of, for example, a family member struggling with a terrible illness, the threat of their company restructuring, or the pressure of adjusting to a newborn at home. And that's what Kaillie and I had to do—push the noise aside and focus on the things that were in our control, on the execution of every step we had to take. We just needed to get back on the ice as soon as possible to realize that it was the same track as before—nothing had changed.

You are very much in the public eye, but what is something you've done that most people wouldn't know about?

I would say that most people know of me because of my sporting career or because they've heard me speak. Those who've heard me speak would know that I have a master's degree in occupational therapy but not that I would have pursued (or chosen) a direction in neuro-rehabilitation. Besides that, very few people (relatively speaking) would know that I used to sing and dance and that I performed in a musical for a summer job right after I graduated from high school. I sang and danced as part of the chorus in a musical all summer for the inauguration of the new Jubilee Theatre in Summerside, P.E.I. I was the youngest cast member (turning eighteen that summer) and only one of two people from P.E.I. who were in the cast. Everyone else either had or was in the process of getting some kind of musical theatre degree, while I was heading into my first year of university to take sciences (an honours degree in kinesiology). It really was an amazing summer—one of my best summers ever!

While your book was in the late stages of production, there was a significant turn of events, so I've got to ask: Why have you decided to return to the sport of bobsleigh leading up to the 2018 PyeongChang Olympic Winter Games after being out of the sport for three-and-a-half years?

Last March (2017), my former teammate Kaillie Humphries asked me if I would push her again this season, and I said no because I'm just not motivated to do the same thing again. I love what I do *now*, and my whole business is focused on helping and empowering *other* people to achieve *their* goals— *their* definition of success.

That being said, early this summer (2017) I was contacted by the high-performance director, who, knowing where I stood on matters, said that *he* was more interested in the idea of me pushing one of the development pilots. I considered the idea, and, to be perfectly frank, it intrigued me. But I just wasn't feeling it—I loved what I was doing (not to mention that I hurt my back in early June and know all too well the physical demands of the sport)—*until* I received an Instagram message from one of the development pilots. She had no idea that discussions with coaches had even taken place but wanted to reach out to see if there was any chance I would consider going back. Besides Kaillie (who has to focus on her own preparation for competition), there are no other girls on the team who have competed in an Olympics Games, and the development pilot (along with the coaching staff) thought that the mindset and experience gained from having competed in high-pressure situations such as various Rugby World Cups and Olympic Games would make a difference in this season. I was impressed with her maturity in recognizing that to compete successfully in those situations takes more than just the physical aspects—the equipment, the push, the drive. Her request wasn't just about me pushing a sled—it was about leadership and mentorship. Guidance in a highly stressful season. And *that* aligns with my messaging and my business: empowering *other* people!

I haven't trained for three-and-a-half years (since the Sochi Olympic Games in 2014). I literally haven't made my body go fast since Sochi, besides racing a friend up a flight of stairs once in 2016 (after which I was sore for two days)! But, as you know, I am also a person who is motivated by challenges, and this is an exciting one for me. Not only is this a chance to see what I am physically capable of (at the age of thirty-nine) but also what I am capable of in terms of my impact on others. My whole business is about empowering *other* people to seize their potential and reach *their* goals. This challenge is about pushing the next generation and investing in Canada's up-and-coming athletes in the bobsleigh program. So, when it comes down to it, my motivation to come back to bobsleigh is *not* because I am excited or inspired at the idea of winning a third Olympic medal. But I *am* motivated and inspired by the thought of potentially helping someone *else* win their *first*.

ACKNOWLEDGEMENTS

ONE OF MY dad's favourite quotes is by Alfred Lord Tennyson: "I am a part of all that I have met." So...
Thank you to every coach, therapist, and teammate I've ever had; to every teacher and classmate; to every neighbour; to every friend; and to every stranger who has crossed my path. Each one of you has taught me something that has made me who I am today.

But more specifically, for this project—for the challenge of testing new waters and writing this book:

Thank you to all those who encouraged me to write it in the first place.

Thanks to Trena White, Carra Simpson, Amanda Lewis, Peter Cocking, and everyone else at Page Two Strategies for the incredible attention to detail and for helping me manoeuvre the publishing industry—guiding me through being a rookie again in a completely new arena. And to my editors, Karen Milner and Heather Sangster, thank you for keeping this book in my voice. It was important for my writing to sound as though I were chatting with a friend in a café, and I am grateful to you both for helping to create that tone.

I couldn't have produced this book without all your brilliant minds, and I'm glad I didn't have to try.

Thank you to Garth Turtle and Dennis Barrett for recognizing the potential in me before I did and for not giving up on my ability to see it for myself. I hope more people take your lead to help others see *their* possibilities, as we are all somewhat limited in our vision by the lens through which we see our lives—a lens created by our surroundings and our experiences.

Thank you so much to Kendra Mills for being my sounding board, especially as the project neared completion. Thank you to Mark Bradley, Hugh Culver, Sam Gibbs, Joe Sherren, and Bruce Rainnie for your perspectives and advice on various aspects of this project. It was comforting to know I had a number of trusted opinions to consider when it came to specific decisions regarding this book. And thanks to Jim Eber for getting me started by helping me pull the stories from my memory.

Thank you to all those who provided testimonials for this book. It means a lot to me that you found value in these pages from which others might benefit.

Thank you to John C. Maxwell for your mentorship and for believing in the impact that I can make, and to Arthur Perlini for our many discussions and your refreshing take on the world.

Thank you to Matt Nichol for teaching me how to thrive as a square peg in a sports world of round holes.

Thank you to my parents for being the best role models a child could ever hope for—for living your lives with morality, integrity, and compassion; for teaching me the value of perspective and to see all sides of an issue; and for imparting on me, by example, the value of making authentic choices. I have often told you that I won't be able to thank you in public for all you've done because my emotion gets caught in my throat. So, I thank you, publicly, now. The only problem is that words really cannot express the love I hold for you in my heart and the gratitude I feel toward you from the depth of my being. I am who I am because of you. And if I can make even *half* as much impact on others as you have made on me, I know that I am making a positive difference in this world.

To Heidi and Walter, you are the best friends anyone could ever hope for. The saying "Siblings by chance, friends by choice" could never be more true. I am blessed to have you both in my life, and I'm so proud and privileged to call you my family.

To my nieces and nephews, thank you for reminding me on a daily basis that there are things that are more important than sports.

To my extended family (blood-related and not), thank you for providing me with homes away from home, for believing in what I do, and for truly being part of this whole journey.

And, finally, thank you to the ceiling-shatterers and barrier-breakers who continue to inspire me. And to the doubters who continue to motivate me.

REFERENCES

Page 10
This quote is a popular adaptation of Bessie Anderson Stanley's poem "Success," More Heart Throbs, vol. 2, ed. Joseph Mitchell Chapple (New York: Grosset & Dunlap, 1911).

Page 26
This quote is attributed most frequently to J.P. Morgan, an American financier and banker; frequently to Chauncey Depew, an American attorney, president of the New York Central Railroad System, and senator; and less frequently to Unknown.

Page 29
Definition available at en.oxforddictionaries.com/definition/potential.

Page 35
John Wooden and Jay Carty, *Coach Wooden's Pyramid of Success: Building Blocks for a Better Life* (Ventura, C: Regal Books, 2005).

Page 43
Albert Einstein.

Page 52
Frank A. Clark, quoted in *The Forbes Book of Business Quotations: 10,000 Thoughts on the Business of Life,* ed. Ted Goodman (New York: Black Dog & Leventhal Publishers, Inc., 2006) 453.

Mark Goffeney, Big Toe Rocks (bigtoerocks.com/). Look for "We Are the Same" and other Mark Goffeney videos on YouTube (www.youtube. com).

Page 53
Scott Barry Kauffman, "What Is Talent—and Can Science Spot What We Will Be Best At?" *The Guardian* (online), July 7, 2013. (Available at www.theguardian.com/science/2013/jul/07/can-science-spot-talent-kaufman.)

Page 59
Jen Sicero, *You Are a Badass: How to Stop Doubting Your Greatness and Start Living an Awesome Life* (Philadelphia: Running Press/Perseus Books Group, 2013).

Page 61
Marianne Williamson, *A Return to Love: Reflections on the Principles of "A Course in Miracles"* (New York: HarperCollins Publishers, 1992), 191.

Page 77
See www.tonyrobbins.com/events/unleash-the-power-within/.

Page 92
See www.facebook.com/thelesbrown/posts/10154099206359654.

Page 100
This quote is attributed most frequently to Stella Stuart; frequently to entrepreneur/author/speaker Mac Anderson; and less frequently to author Carl (Tuchy) Palmieri and Unknown.

Page 110
Although the original source for this quote is likely Unknown, Arnold Schwarzenegger made it popular.

Page 111
This quote is most recently and frequently attributed to entrepreneur/author/speaker Ryan Blair, although entrepreneur/author/speaker Jim Rohn, actor Frank Banks, and Unknown have also been credited.

Page 125
Walter Anderson.

Page 128
Dr. Seuss, *Oh, The Places You'll Go!* (New York: Random House Children's Books, 1960).

Page 139
Stephen R. Covey, *The Wisdom and Teachings of Stephen R. Covey* (New York: Free Press/Simon & Schuster, Inc., 2012).

Page 153
See johnmaxwell.podbean.com/?s=potential.

Page 158
Although this quote has been frequently attributed to Michelangelo since the late 1990s, it has not been found before 1983, when it appeared without attribution in E.C. McKenzie's *Mac's Giant Book of Quips and Quotes* (Grand Rapids, MI: Baker Book House, 1983). (See en.wikiquote.org/wiki/Michelangelo.)

Page 159
See www.pbs.org/newshour/updates/military-julydec11-ptsd_12-06/; www.eomega.org/article/the-great-ptsd-name-debate; saveoursoldier. co.uk/ptsi/; toronto.citynews.ca/2016/11/10/post-traumatic-stress-injury-notdisorder-veterans-say/; www.posttraumaticstressinjury. org/; and globalptsifoundation.org/ptsd-vs-ptsi.

Page 168
Jack Canfield with Janet Switzer, *The Success Principles: How to Get from Where You Are to Where You Want to Be* (New York: HarperCollins Publishers, 2005).

Page 170
Simon Sinek. (startwithwhy.com)

Page 185
Stephen R. Covey, *The 7 Habits of Highly Effective People* (New York: Free Press/Simon & Schuster, Inc., 1989).

Laura Vanderkam, "How to Gain Control of Your Free Time,"
TED Talks/TEDwomen, October 2016. (See www.ted.com/talks/
laura_vanderkam_how_to_gain_control_of_your_free_time.)

Page 199
Angela Duckworth, *Grit: The Power of Passion and Perseverance*
(New York: Scribner/Simon & Schuster, Inc., 2016).

Page 206
Dr. Carol S. Dweck, *Mindset: The New Psychology of Success* (New
York: Random House, 2006).

PHOTO CREDITS

THE AUTHOR GRATEFULLY acknowledges the permission granted to reproduce the copyright material in this book. Every effort has been made to trace copyright holders and to obtain their permission for the use of copyright material. The author apologizes for any errors or omissions and would be grateful if notified of any corrections that should be incorporated in future reprints or editions of this book.

Jacket cover photos (front and back)
Mark MacLean

Promo page photo
Christian Del Rosario

HEATHER'S PHOTO ALBUM

Page 1
All courtesy of the author

Page 2
All courtesy of the author, except for the portrait with parents:
Heckberts Studio

Page 3
All courtesy of the author

Page 4
TOP: Paul Seiser/SPA Images
BOTTOM: Jordan Verlage

Page 5
TOP: Paul Seiser/SPA Images
MIDDLE: Paul Seiser/SPA Images
RIGHT, TOP: Ron LeBlanc
RIGHT, BOTTOM: Courtesy of the author

Page 6
TOP: Courtesy of the author
BOTTOM LEFT: Charlie Booker
BOTTOM RIGHT: THE CANADIAN PRESS/Jonathan Hayward

Page 7
TOP ROW, CLOCKWISE FROM L: Canadian Olympic Committee/
Winston Chow; Canadian Olympic Committee/Jason Ransom; THE
CANADIAN PRESS/Adrian Wyld
MIDDLE ROW, L TO R: Courtesy of the author; courtesy of the author;
photographer unknown
BOTTOM ROW, L TO R: Courtesy of the author; Canadian Olympic
Committee/Dave Sandford

Page 8
All courtesy of the author, except for the World Rugby Hall of Fame
photos: World Rugby/Getty Images

Page 9
FROM TOP TO BOTTOM: Courtesy of the author; courtesy of the
author; Canadian Olympic Committee/Jonathan Hayward; THE
CANADIAN PRESS/Jeff McIntosh

Page 10
TOP: Event photographer for Hofburg Sylvester Ball (New Year's Eve
2016) at the Hofburg Palace, Vienna, Australia
MIDDLE: Courtesy of the author
BOTTOM, L AND R: Courtesy of the author

Page 11
All courtesy of the author

Page 12
TOP: Photographer unknown
MIDDLE: Courtesy of the author
BOTTOM: Courtesy of the author

Page 13
CLOCKWISE FROM TOP LEFT: Twitter/photographer unknown; Kevin
D. Liles; courtesy of Rogers Hometown Hockey; Michelle Valberg;
courtesy of the author

Page 14
CLOCKWISE FROM TOP LEFT: Courtesy of the author; Kristian
Bogner; Kristian Bogner; courtesy of the author

Page 15
All courtesy of the author

Page 16
All courtesy of the author, except for *The Hour* photo: courtesy of
George Stroumboulopoulos

ABOUT THE AUTHOR

THREE-TIME OLYMPIAN AND two-time Olympic gold medallist Heather Moyse is a multi-sport athlete and now a highly respected motivational speaker. She's competed internationally in track cycling, rugby, *and* bobsleigh, in which she and her teammate won gold at the Vancouver 2010 and Sochi 2014 Winter Olympic Games. In 2016, Heather was the first Canadian female, and only the second Canadian *ever,* to be inducted into the World Rugby Hall of Fame.

Heather uses her personal experiences—and professional training as an occupational therapist—to encourage and inspire *others* to embrace challenges and face adversities head-on, to believe in the possibilities of achieving their dreams, and to fulfill their potential whether in sports, business, or life. To further personally embrace these points, Heather also summited the highest mountain in Antarctica in January 2016 with a group that included eight members of the Canadian Armed Forces to raise awareness for post-traumatic stress disorder. As a lifelong humanitarian, Heather donates her time and talent to many community events and national charities, earning her the Order of Prince Edward Island, the Diamond Jubilee Medal, and the Randy Starkman Olympian Humanitarian Award.

"

Believe in the possibilities! We are all capable of *way more* than we give ourselves credit for!

"

To some, "believe in the possibilities" is an inspirational quote, but for Heather Moyse, it's a way of life. As a three-sport national athlete and two-time Olympic gold medallist, Heather is an inspiration to many. Having overcome multiple career-threatening injuries, she uses her personal experience as an athlete—and her professional training as an occupational therapist—to encourage and empower *others* to embrace challenges and face adversity head-on; to believe in the possibilities of achieving their dreams; and to step outside of their comfort zones to discover and maximize their potential whether it be in sports, business, or life. Heather's record of excellence has afforded her a unique perspective and understanding, which she conveys through an engaging presentation.

What Clients Have Said After
Hearing Heather Speak . . .

"Heather's presentation was definitely a critical success factor for our event, and we would highly recommend her for any events that require a speaker who can deliver the wow factor."

PETER L. TIERNEY, Fisher & Paykel Appliances

"Heather's personal journey toward Olympic gold is a story that should be heard by anyone who aspires to excellence. Her engaging presentation and stories outlining her relentless drive to overcome obstacles were well-received by our team and provided a highly motivating tone to our meeting. Many of our team members cited her speech as a highlight of the conference."

BRAD FLETCHER, Managing Director, Brown-Forman Canada

". . . It was her message's relevance to our advisors that far surpassed our expectation! Heather is a shining example of setting goals, perseverance, determination, and overcoming obstacles, all of which relate to a business setting... My only regret is that we didn't give her more time on stage for a longer Q & A session. I would highly recommend hiring Heather for any event if you want to motivate and impress!"

GREG FOX, Regional Manager, Sun Life Financial

To see a list of Heather's previous clients for speaking engagements, please visit:

www.heathermoyse.com/keynote-speaker

Book Heather Now

If you're hosting an event, a meeting, or a conference that you believe could use a touch of Heather Moyse's perspective, meaning you want your team to believe in the possibilities and take themselves and your organization to the next level—don't wait! Whether it's for a speaking engagement, appearance, or other event request, please visit **www.heathermoyse.com /contact** or email **info@heathermoyse.com** because not only would Heather add the wow factor you're looking for, she would also love to help.

Are you feeling stuck in your life? Finding it difficult to see the path from where you are now to where you want to be? Heather wrote this book as a way of impacting more people, but if you are wanting more, please reach out. Although Heather doesn't actively promote herself as a personal coach/mentor, as that is not her primary approach to helping people seize their potential, she has worked one-on-one with individuals* who were feeling stuck, unmotivated, or just in need of some help to shift their perspective so they could see the possibilities in their lives. For more information, please visit www.heathermoyse.com or email info@heathermoyse.com.

*Heather takes on only two individual clients at a time in order to ensure quality service delivery.

Could someone you know benefit from **Redefining 'Realistic'?**

Redefining 'Realistic' is the perfect gift for anyone who needs to see their situation in a different way—a shift in perspective allows them to see the possibilities that exist within their circumstance. Giving this book shows you care, shows that you see their potential and believe in what they are truly capable of.

For an order of ten or more books, we offer a discount. Please write to us for details at:

bookqueries@heathermoyse.com.

EARLY DAYS

TOP I started training early, without even realizing it.

LEFT TOP My older sister, Heidi, and me bringing our new puppy, Princess Heischeawa, home. Her name is made up of letters from the first names of all my immediate family members.

LEFT BOTTOM Leave it to a Prince Edward Island kid to bury her younger brother (Walter) in a basket of potatoes.

BOTTOM RIGHT This Easter photo perfectly captures our sibling dynamic (Walter, me in the middle, and Heidi)

FAMILY

RUGBY

I feel extremely lucky to have been able to play a sport I love so much on the international stage at the 2006 (Canada) and 2010 (England) Women's Rugby World Cups and at the 2013 Rugby World Cup Sevens (Russia).

vancou
2010

OLYMPICS

TOP Standing with English player Maggie Alphonsi before the official ceremony in which we were the only two females inducted into the World Rugby Hall of Fame in 2016. Maggie and I played against each other on a number of occasions.

RIGHT My family cottage is probably my favourite place on earth. No TV. No Internet. No insulation. Just family, chipmunks, birds . . . and peace. It's where I recharge my batteries.

BELOW Doing pool rehab in a *very* 'attractive' flotation suit a month after my November 21, 2012, hip surgery.

BELIEVING IN THE POSSIBILITIES

FROM TOP TO BOTTOM

My teammate Helen Upperton and me at the Opening Ceremony for the 2006 Winter Olympic Games in Turin (Torino), Italy.

Standing in a sea of colourful team jackets as the athletes leave the Stadio Olimpico after the Torino 2006 Opening Ceremony.

Helen and me setting push-start records on the Torino Olympics bobsleigh track in Sestriere, Italy.

With teammates (*l to r*) Kaillie Humphries, Helen Upperton, and Shelley-Ann Brown as we display our gold and silver 2010 Winter Olympic (Vancouver) medals moments after stepping off the podium.

LEFT My parents and my Aunt Roberta and Uncle Alex, who joined my parents on their bucket-list trip to waltz their way into 2017 in Vienna, Austria.

BELOW With John C. Maxwell—one of the best and most kind-hearted human beings on the planet. I feel fortunate that he's a mentor of mine, and even more so because he sees the potential impact I can make on the world.

OPPORTUNITIES & ADVENTURES

ABOVE Pushing my brother in neutral for training made pushing bobsleds seem much easier.

OPPOSITE TOP The gym was closed one day while I was visiting my parents in P.E.I. during summer 2009. *Soo . . .* just had to get a bit creative. #NoExcusesNoRegrets

OPPOSITE BOTTOM Since there were no bathtubs in the Mountain Village at the 2014 Sochi Winter Olympic Games, I took my scheduled Epsom salts bath in an empty recycling bin! Again . . . just had to get a bit creative. ☺

MORE OPPORTUNITIES & ADVENTURES

TOP The 2012 Pan American Track Cycling Championships in Mar del Plata, Argentina, was my first international race. Actually . . . my first race *ever!*

LEFT My sister, Heidi, convinced me to play rugby again in summer 2004 with the enticing argument that it would be fun to play on the same team again . . . *Bam!* Not only did we play together, but we bonded with matching black eyes. LOL.

BELOW My pet duck, Rugger. It only took him (or her?) three-and-a-half months to grow from a duckling to full feathers. I wanted to bring Rugger back to Canada in 2002, but the quarantine would have killed him. So when I left Trinidad, I gave him to a *vegetarian* family! ☺

There are ups and downs in every race/game, but we are proof that if you keep believing in the possibilities, results can be golden. Own it! The ice is YOURS! Fight 'til the bitter end!

Smiles...

Heather + Kaillie

ABOVE The note I wrote to the Canadian women's hockey team before their final game at the 2014 Sochi Winter Olympics. It's not something I would ever have thought of taking a picture of, but I found this photo later on Twitter. LOL!

FROM TOP TO BOTTOM

Speaking on stage with John C. Maxwell for his Live 2 Lead simulcast to 35,000-plus people. I discussed my new book (*this* book) and my reason for returning to the sport of bobsledding after such a long hiatus to help an up-and-coming driver get to her first Olympics.

With (*l to r*) Ron MacLean, Doug MacLean (no, they're not related), and Tara Slone doing a *Rogers Hometown Hockey* segment in Summerside, P.E.I. Always fun to work with amazing people.

Had the pleasure of travelling to Baffin Island, Nunavut, to visit a couple of communities, meet some of the locals, and learn more about their culture and the environment. I found out that I was the first Olympian ever to visit Clyde River (photo) and Pond Inlet. Sitting with me and the kids is Mylène Paquette, who rowed solo across the North Atlantic Ocean in 2013. It was wonderful to share this Arctic experience with such a great person.

After an event with two of P.E.I.'s most recognized and loved people: Bruce Rainnie (*l*) and Kevin "Boomer" Gallant (*r*). The *CBC News: Compass* duo served as anchor and weather specialist, respectively, entering the living rooms and hearts of Islanders together every dinner hour for thirteen-and-a-half years until they both retired in April 2017.

ANTARCTICA

EVEN MORE OPPORTUNITIES & ADVENTURES

1ST ROW With George Stroumboulopoulos on *The Hour*.

2ND ROW (*l to r*) Scotland and Baffin Island.

3RD ROW (*l to r*) With Michael "Pinball" Clemons, at the Boat Rally for Kids with Cancer, with Right to Play in West Africa.

OPPOSITE I love that my job now is to empower others.